The Concept of Soul in Judaism, Christianity and Islam

Key Concepts in Interreligious Discourses

Edited by
Georges Tamer

Volume 11

The Concept of Soul in Judaism, Christianity and Islam

Edited by
Christoph Böttigheimer and
Wenzel Maximilian Widenka

DE GRUYTER

ISBN 978-3-11-074818-5
e-ISBN (PDF) 978-3-11-074823-9
e-ISBN (EPUB) 978-3-11-074827-7
ISSN 2513-1117

Library of Congress Control Number: 2023935164

Bibliographic information published by the Deutsche Nationalbibliothek
The Deutsche Nationalbibliothek lists this publication in the Deutsche Nationalbibliografie; detailed bibliographic data are available on the internet at http://dnb.dnb.de.

Typesetting: Integra Software Services Pvt. Ltd.
Printing and binding: CPI books GmbH, Leck

www.degruyter.com

Preface

This volume at hand of the book series "Key Concepts in Interreligious Discourses" (KCID) documents the results of a conference which dealt with the concept of "Soul" in Judaism, Christianity and Islam and was held at the Catholic University of Eichstätt-Ingolstadt. The conference was organised by the research unit "Key Concepts in Interreligious Discourses" and took place June 26–June 28, 2019.

The research unit "Key Concepts in Interreligious Discourses" was jointly run by the Friedrich-Alexander-University Erlangen-Nuremberg and the Catholic University Eichstätt-Ingolstadt between June 2018 and June 2021. As the title already implies, the mutual project focused on interreligious discourse. Its aim was to reflect upon and thereby facilitate a theologically well-founded interreligious dialogue. For only if every dialogue partner has a clear picture of what is discussed, a dialogue can be conducted reasonably. It was the project's ambition to provide such clarification by examining concepts that are central for Judaism, Christianity and Islam, both historically and in terms of their interdependencies and by setting them in a relation to one another. By reflecting on central ideas and beliefs historically and comparatively, common values and origins, but also differences and contradictions between the three monotheistic religions are to be clearly elaborated. By disclosing key concepts of the three closely interconnected religions: Judaism, Christianity and Islam, a deeper mutual understanding is fostered, prejudices and misunderstandings are counteracted and thus a contribution is made to peaceful interaction based on respect and recognition.

Only through precise knowledge of the central ideas of the foreign as well as of one's own religion a well-founded, objective and constructive interreligious understanding can prevail. Conferences at which international experts from the fields of theology, religious studies and philosophy of religion intensively discussed and clarified core religious ideas from the perspective of the three religions served this purpose. Developments within religious history never proceed in isolation; rather, they interpenetrate each other and are mutually dependent. Thus, the research unit "Key Concepts in Interreligious Discourses" pursued fundamental research and aimed at an "archaeology of knowledge" with its comparative conceptual-historical investigations.

Inasmuch as world peace cannot be obtained without religious peace, the project contributed importantly to a peaceful social coexistence and thus corresponds to the obligation that has been newly assigned to the universities in recent decades, namely to engage in social concerns in addition to teaching and research. This is expressed by the term "third mission".

I wish to thank Dr. Wenzel Maximilian Widenka, who not only organised the conference but also edited this volume. In addition to the cooperation partners of

https://doi.org/10.1515/9783110748239-202

the Friedrich-Alexander-University Erlangen-Nuremberg and the de Gruyter publishing house for including this volume in the book series "Key Concepts in Interreligious Discourses", we would like to express our sincere thanks to the third party funders, Reinhard Cardinal Marx and the archdiocese of Munich-Freising, the Karpos Foundation of the Diocese Eichstätt, the Maximilian Bickhoff Foundation and the ProFor Program of the Catholic University Eichstätt-Ingolstadt. Without their support, neither the conference nor the volumes would have been possible.

This volume is dedicated to Prof. Dr. Eberhard Schockenhoff, who died unexpectedly not long after the conference.

Christoph Böttigheimer,
June 2022

Contents

Preface — V

Alan J. Avery-Peck
The Concept of Soul in Judaism — 1

Eberhard Schockenhoff
The Concept of Soul in Christianity — 21

Bernhard Uhde
The Concept of Soul in Islam — 67

Christoph Böttigheimer and Wenzel M. Widenka
Epilogue — 115

List of Contributors and Editors — 127

Index of Persons — 129

Index of Subjects — 131

Alan J. Avery-Peck

The Concept of Soul in Judaism

Prologue

Humans quite naturally see themselves as bifurcated beings, distinguishing between physical attributes – the body – and our expressive selves, represented most obviously in the power of cognition. The idea of this division is a natural outcome of our day-to-day experience of ourselves. Our minds and bodies often seem to operate, and so to exist, independently of each other. Our thoughts, imagination, dreams, longings, and other emotions frequently are experienced separately from our physical body and its activities. On the other side, our body and limbs often seem to engage in rote behaviors without any clear connection to conscious thought. And then there is the question of life itself. We imagine our bodies to be the containers for a life force that comprises more than mere chemical processes. Upon death, the body remains, and it is hard for us to imagine that the life force and cognition that once animated us do not somehow also continue to exist.

This sense of a bifurcation between the physical body and the life force leads in almost every culture and religion to a conception of what we call the soul. To state what perhaps should be obvious, this means that, when we speak of the soul, we are speaking of the reification of an intellectual construction of the self. This being the case, we must always be conscious of the ways in which any particular idea of the soul responds to the distinctive needs and perspectives of the individuals and communities that develop and use that particular conception.

In the following, I illustrate this point by tracking the development of the idea of the soul from the Hebrew Bible and into the rabbinic Judaism that, in the first centuries C.E., reimagined all prior Jewish thought and practice. My point is that, to understand the idea of the soul in Judaism, we must understand the perspectives and experiences of the rabbis who, in the first centuries, created that idea. I argue, this is to say, that the diverse and often conflicting conceptions of the soul that emerge over time in Judaism are explained by the social and political contexts, by the theological and communal needs of the people who in each age developed their own particular idea of the soul. In imagining the soul, the rabbis made choices. The question for us is how those choices responded to their distinctive needs within their particular historical reality. How did the rabbis' conception of the soul fit within and advance their program for Judaism? To answer this question, we begin by assessing the concept of the soul in the Hebrew Bible, the baseline against which we can then consider what is new in the rabbis' thinking.

https://doi.org/10.1515/9783110748239-001

In following this approach, I do not mean to ignore the diverse developments in thinking about the soul that occurred across a range of manifestations of Judaism before rabbinic times: in the intertestamental literatures, in the writings of the Dead Sea Sect, in authors such as Philo, and, contemporaneously with the emergence of rabbinism, in early Christianity. These developments, alongside ideas about the soul found in Hellenistic cultures that were familiar to the rabbis, likely had an impact on rabbinic thinking. But their existence does not explain the choices the rabbis made in their distinctive presentation of the soul. To date, the scholarly preference has been for comparative research on ideas about the soul in the range of early manifestations of Judaism. My focus is more limited: to evaluate how the rabbis' idea of the soul advanced rabbinic thinking as they made sense of the changed and disrupted world within which they lived. For our purposes, we can profitably move from the Hebrew Bible directly to the rabbinic literature, even as we are conscious of the diverse Jewish and non-Jewish sources on which the rabbis might have drawn.[1]

1 The Soul in the Hebrew Bible

The Hebrew Bible offers an extremely narrow definition of and almost total lack of knowledge of the soul. This is striking because, within many ancient near-eastern cultures, the soul was known and was broadly associated with traits such as physical appearance, destiny, and power.[2] In ancient Israel, by contrast, rather than being seen as an aspect of identity, what later translations render as soul primarily referred to respiration, narrowly signifying the life force. This is reflected in the root meanings of the several Hebrew words that often are translated as soul. Thus we find the words *nefesh* ("breath"), *neshamah* ("breathing"), and *ruach* (literally, "wind"). Having to do primarily with respiration, these terms encompass the Latin words for soul: *anima*, which is close to the Hebrew concept of *ruach*; and *spiritus*, which parallels the Hebrew terms *nefesh* and *neshamah*. At the same time, as we shall see, in Scripture, what these words represent hardly goes

1 For overviews, see Finney, Mark T., *Resurrection, Hell and the Afterlife: Body and Soul in Antiquity, Judaism and Early Christianity*, New York: Routledge, 2016, and Segal, Alan F., *Life after Death: The History of the Afterlife in Western Religion*, New York: Doubleday, 2004.

2 On concepts of the soul in the ancient near east, see Steiner, Richard C., *Disembodied Souls: The Nefesh in Israel and Kindred Spirits in the Ancient Near East, with an Appendix on the Katumuwa Inscription*, Universidad Católica Argentina Centro de Estudios de Historia del Antiguo Oriente: SBL Press, 2015.

beyond the words' most basic implication: people's respiration, the fact that they are breathing, signifies that they are alive.

The Hebrew Bible connects this life-force to God's own *ruach*, that is, the "spirit," "wind," or "breath" from God that Gen 1:2 describes as moving over the face of the waters at the time of God's creation of the world. That same word, *ruach*, appears 33 times in Scripture, referring to the breath of a person's mouth or nostrils. Notably though, while the breath that gives Adam, the first man, life explicitly comes from God, it is described using not this word – *ruach* – but the other terms that Scripture generally associates with respiration. Gen 2:7 states: "Then the Lord God formed man of dust from the ground, and breathed into his nostrils the breath of life (*nishmat hayyim*); and man became a living being (*nefesh hayyah*)." So the *ruach* of God that animates creation is not in Scripture the same "breath," and certainly not the same "soul," that animates the first man.[3]

It bears noting that, alongside breath, Scripture connects the life-force to blood, which accounts for the prohibition against eating meat from which all blood has not been drained, as at Gen 9:4, among other similar verses. This association also accounts for the important function of the blood of sacrifices. In sacrifice, the animal's blood has expiatory power, as Lev 17:11 makes explicit: "For the life-force (*nefesh*) of the flesh is in the blood; and I have given it for you upon the altar to make atonement for yourself/your life-force (*nefesh*); for it is the blood that makes atonement, by reason of the life-force (*nefesh*)." The destruction of the animal's life-force saves from destruction the parallel life-force of the human on behalf of whom the offering is made.

We see here the biblical understanding of living beings as split, comprised of a physical body that is earthly and a life force that at least arguably is divine in origin, having been breathed into the first human by God. Still, we need to be clear that this perception does not represent a biblical idea of what we might define as a soul. In Scripture, the same life-force exists in all living creatures, animals as much as people, and it neither pre-exists birth nor continues to exist after death. Beyond its presence in the body as an animating force, it has no independent existence or power. It is not what we would call a soul.

That this is the case is suggested most strongly by the fact that Scripture also uses the term *nefesh* simply to designate a person him- or herself. In this usage, the term may stand for the essential substance of the human being, the person's emotions, passions, appetite and, on occasion, knowledge. The *nefesh* feels love

3 Just as life is marked by the presence of breath in the body, death is understood to occur when this breath (*nefesh*) leaves the body. Describing the death of the matriarch Rachel during childbirth, Gen 35:18 makes the point explicit: "And as her breath/soul (*nefesh*) was departing (for she died), she called his name Ben-o'ni . . . ."

and longs for another person (Gen 34:3);[4] it experiences distress (Gen 42:21);[5] and it is the seat of true knowledge, e.g., of God, as at Deut 11:18.[6]

But even in such usages, this term, though commonly translated soul, may be nothing more than the biblical author's way of referring to the person him- or herself. This is clear, for instance, at Exod 1:5, which states, "All the offspring of Jacob were seventy *nefashot,*" that is, seventy people.[7] Given this use of the term, it is perhaps not surprising to find that Ps 11:5 can even depict God as having a "*nefesh*:" "The Lord tests the righteous and the wicked, and his *nefesh* hates him that loves violence." The *nefesh*, that is, is the sum and substance of the being, whether a person or even God. But it is not more than that. It thus should be clear that, despite the common biblical use of the term *nefesh*, Scripture does not present even a rudimentarily developed concept of the soul in any sense familiar to today's common definition. All life, as the creation narrative makes clear, originates with God. But the Hebrew Scriptures offer no specific ideas pointing to the existence of individual, independent souls that preexist birth, that exist separate from respiration during life, or that outlive the death of the body.

Explaining why a literature – or the social and religious system that literature represents – lacks any particular ideology is fraught. At the same time, a few comments regarding the absence of the concept of a soul in the Hebrew Bible are in order. For, just as I will argue is the case for the rabbinic literature, Scripture's perspective – or lack of a viewpoint – on the soul tallies with its distinctive perception of life. The Hebrew Bible, in almost all of its diverse writings, expresses confidence that life – including the good and the bad, the apparent rewards and punishments – is exclusively a matter of the world in which we now live and of the life span of each individual. The most we humans should expect for following God's demands is a long life. Immortality, in this view, is found in the continuation of our family line, represented in our progeny. But when we are dead, in the Hebrew Bible's view, we are in fact dead. End of story.

---

4 "And [Shechem's] soul (*nefesh*) was drawn to Dinah the daughter of Jacob; he loved the maiden and spoke tenderly to her."

5 Joseph's brother's report: ". . . we saw the distress of his [our brother's] soul, when he besought us and we would not listen."

6 *NRSV:* "You shall put these words of mine in your heart and soul, and you shall bind them as a sign on your hand, and fix them as an emblem on your forehead." Notably, in this verse, NIV explicitly translates *nefesh* as "minds."

7 See similarly Exod 31:14: "whoever does any work on it [that is, the Sabbath], that *nefesh* shall be cut off from among his people." The term refers to the person him or herself, in the sense of, "that living being."

In this context, the idea of a soul that predates a person's birth or continues to exist after death is not only philosophically unworkable but theologically and socially unnecessary. We get what we deserve during the course of our lives, and going to our deaths at a ripe old age is the only reward we can expect or need. Notably, the two places in Scripture that evidence a more developed thinking about the soul and life-after-death emerge in the latest period of biblical history, during the Babylonian exile and, still later, in the aftermath of the Maccabean revolt. These are periods that challenged the idea that God's justice is experienced during our lifetime. Ecclesiastes, written in the third century B.C.E., distinctively within Scripture questions the order and justice of the world. In the context of such questioning, the idea of a soul, the immortality of which might justify the suffering that people experience during their bodily life, makes sense. And indeed, Ecclesiastes is the one place in the Hebrew Bible that seems to know of such an idea, even if it expresses uncertainty regarding the soul's actual existence (Eccl 3:19–21):

> For the fate of humans and the fate of animals is the same; as one dies, so dies the other. They all have the same spirit (*ruach*), and humans have no advantage over the animals; for all is vanity. All go to one place; all are from the dust, and all turn to dust again. Who knows whether the human spirit (*ruach*) goes upward and the spirit of animals goes downward to the earth?

In exactly the historical context in which we would imagine a concept of the soul to become theologically useful in the Hebrew Bible, it appears – even if it remains undeveloped and subject to questioning. The notion of the soul as an independent force that animates human life and that exists apart from the human body thus is developed only in later Judaisms. My argument is that, as in the period of the book of Ecclesiastes, so in the tribulations of the world of the rabbis, a conception of an independent soul became useful, even necessary. The idea of the soul helped the rabbis explain the apparently unjust and even God-devoid world that they confronted. While we cannot ignore the fact that an idea of the soul had increasingly been known in intertestamental Judaism, in the rabbinic period this conception firmly enters the religious system that shaped all later Jewish belief and practice.

2 The Soul in Rabbinic Judaism

In order to understand rabbinic thinking about the soul in the context of the world in which the rabbis lived, we begin by delineating that world.[8] The rabbis' reality can be outlined rather starkly:

1. Rabbinic Judaism was conceived in the land of Israel in the period following the Jewish revolt against Rome that, in the first century C.E., led to the destruction of the Jerusalem Temple. That Temple was the epicenter of the Jewish worship of God and the only place in which the divinely mandated sacrificial cult could take place. Save for an eighty year period following its destruction by Nebuchadnezzar of Babylonia in 586 B.C.E., the Temple had stood and its cult operated since its construction under King Solomon, a thousand years before.
2. The rabbinic program for Judaism was shaped in the immediate aftermath of the devastating second Jewish revolt against Rome of 132–135 C.E. This revolt was led by Bar Kokhba, whose followers declared him the messiah, that is, the anointed leader sent by God to fulfill the promise of a reinstated Davidic monarchy. The outcome instead was as many as half a million Jews dead and Jerusalem's being turned into a Roman colony, with a temple of Jupiter Capitolinus erected on the Temple Mount.
3. Rabbinic Judaism gained control over the Jewish nation in the 4th–6th centuries C.E., the period of the firm establishment of Christianity as the official religion of the Roman world.

The destruction of the Temple, the failed Bar Kokhba revolt, and the ascent of Christianity potentially meant the end of the Jews' perception of their destiny as a great and holy nation – the chosen people. The destruction of the Temple and its replacement with a pagan shrine meant that there could be no possible expectation of the Temple's being rebuilt or of a return to the way things had been before. And the success of Christianity, with its claim to embody a new covenant that superseded that of God with the Jews, meant that even the notion of Israel's chosenness and unique relationship to God was subject to significant challenge.

In these ways, both the political and theological contexts in which Judaism existed and in which Jews lived were dramatically altered. As a result of the events of the first centuries, the Jewish people, whether in the land of Israel or, now, largely in diaspora, had lost the symbols of their power, the sign of their

---

8 On the history of Judaism in this period, see Goldenberg, Robert, *The Origins of Judaism: From Canaan to the Rise of Islam*, Cambridge: Cambridge University Press, 2007, 120–178. See also Stemberger, Günter, "The Formation of Rabbinic Judaism, 70–640 CE," in: Jacob Neusner / Alan Avery-Peck (eds.), *The Blackwell Companion to Judaism*, Malden / Oxford: Blackwell Publishing, 2003, 78–92.

place among the nations, and the physical representation of their stature before God. In this context, new thinking about the nature of the body and the finality of death needed to take place. And within rabbinic Judaism, exactly such thinking emerged.

Overall, the new rabbinic ideology responded to the disasters of the first centuries by refocusing the people of Israel's concerns from the events of political history, which are, after all, far beyond the control of the individual, to events within the life and control of each person and family. What came to matter were the every-day details of life, the recurring actions that, day-in and day-out, define who we are and demarcate what is truly important to us. In this process, Judaism became a religion of law and practice, focused on how people live their life in this world. At the same time, the rabbis hardly gave up on the dream of the rebuilding of the Temple, the re-establishment of animal sacrifice, the ingathering of the exiles, and renewed Israelite sovereignty. What changed was that now they argued that these things would be achieved only when the people of Israel were truly deserving of this reward and, even then, through God's direct intervention in history, in the creation of a messianic age-to-come, not as aspects of this world.

Rabbinic ideology was therefore in many regards paradoxical. It told people to focus on their lives and behaviors in this world. And yet it asserted that the ultimate value of what people do in this world is that it assures them a place in a utopian world-to-come. As part of this thinking about a future divine reward, the rabbis needed entirely to reconsider the nature of human life. If no recompense for proper behavior could be anticipated in this world, it was no longer sufficient to imagine that death was the end of everything. In this context the rabbis focused on the soul, which would survive death and enjoy the rewards that had eluded the person during this-worldly life. The concept of the soul thus entered rabbinic Judaism as part and parcel of the rabbinic program for the survival of Judaism amid the realities of the world the rabbis of the first centuries experienced.

The point is that, unlike in the Hebrew Bible, in the Talmudic literature, in sources dated from the fourth to the sixth centuries C.E., the soul is seen as an independent creation, distinct from the body and separate from simple respiration. Now it is understood to preexist the body into which it is placed and to exist apart from the body after death. This means that there is more to life than immediately meets the eye, a different reality that portrays God's justice and larger plan for the people of Israel. And yet, as we shall see, in keeping with their this-worldly and non-messianic focus, the rabbis of the Talmudic literature are also explicit that the soul neither has priority over the body nor is to be valorized as the aspect of the bifurcated human being that most matters. In rabbinic ideology, this is to say, the body and soul stand in necessary connection to each other. Just as the body absent the soul has no life, so the soul, absent the body, has no meaningful existence, neither in relationship to God nor to the world.

Rabbinic authorities thus do not conceive of the soul's immortality separate from the *eventual* immortality of the body. Nor do they imagine a transmigration of the soul from one body to another. Body and soul, rather, are understood as separate only in origin, with the body deriving from human parents and the soul originating with God. In practice, the soul, created and bestowed upon the body by God, is taken back to God at death. But at the time of the resurrection – another idea that is absent from Scripture but that the rabbis make a central tenet of their religion – the soul will be restored to that same body, with this reunified person standing in final judgment before God.[9] Before we assess the implications of this perspective for rabbinic thinking overall, let us examine the details.

In developing their concept of the soul, the rabbis use the language and basic ideas of Scripture regarding the soul's role in respiration, its being the seat of the individual's character, and its standing in close relationship to God.[10] Where the rabbis move well beyond Scripture is in defining the soul as more than simply respiration, that is, in holding that it exists separate and apart from the body. The rabbis understand all human souls to have been brought into existence during God's creation of the universe, as aspects of the wind or spirit (*ruach*) of God referred to at Gen 1:2. In line with this assertion, the rabbis understand that the messiah cannot come and God's covenantal promises cannot be fulfilled until all the souls prepared at the time of creation have been used. Babylonian Talmud Abodah Zarah 5a makes the point as follows:[11]

> And said R. Yose, "The son of David will come only when all of the souls that are stored up in the *Guf*[12] will be used up. [This is proven by the verse]: 'For I will not continually accuse, neither will I be always angry, that the spirit (*ruach*) should fall before me and the souls (*neshamot*) that I have made' (Is 57:16)."

While the way in which Yose reads the cited verse from Isaiah is hardly clear, the point is apparent: God's plan for the universe and the people in it was established at creation. All people who were ever to be born were anticipated at that time, stored up in the *Guf*. Only when those people all have been brought to life can the completion of God's plan, marked by the restoration of the Davidic monarchy,

9 Alongside the texts cited below, see, e.g., Talmud Yerushalmi Kilaim 8:4, 31c, and Babylonian Talmud Berakhot 60a.

10 See in particular Genesis Rabbah 14:9.

11 Translations of the Babylonian Talmud are adapted from Neusner, Jacob, *The Babylonian Talmud: A Translation and Commentary*, Peabody: Hendrickson Publishers, 2011.

12 Literally, "body." See Jastrow, Marcus, *Dictionary of the Targumim, Talmud Babli, Yerushalmi and Midrashic Literature*, New York: Judaica Press, reprint, 1971, 225, s.v., *gwp*.

come about. The implication is that, despite what we are now experiencing in the world, God's plan is in motion and will lead to the fulfillment of God's promises. This additionally suggests that even God cannot simply go ahead and immediately bring about the messianic kingdom. This can occur only when God's entire plan, set out at the time of creation, is fulfilled. The rabbis' thinking about the existence of souls thus supports their larger world view: do what is right and, in due course, God will take care of the rest.

In another Talmudic passage, Simeon b. Laqish imagines the heavens to be comprised of seven firmaments. Explaining the nature of the firmament referred to as "the heavy cloud," Babylonian Talmud Haggigah 12b develops the idea of the preexistence of souls:

> "Heavy cloud:" that is where there are right, judgment, and righteousness, the treasures of life and the treasures of peace and the treasures of blessing, the souls (*neshamot*) of the righteous and the spirits (*ruachot*) and souls that are yet to be born, and dew with which the Holy One, blessed be he, in the age to come will revive the dead.

The soul, in Talmudic thought, exists in heaven prior to the conception of the corporeal body in which it will be placed, and the souls of the righteous similarly return to heaven following the death of the body with which they had been associated. But, as is suggested here, the end plan is not for those unembodied souls to continue to exist in heaven. It is, rather, the eventual resurrection of the dead through the reuniting of bodies and their souls.

This means that, despite its separate origin, the soul's destiny is tied directly to that of the body. A highly developed depiction of the relationship between soul and body appears in the 5th–7th century compilation Tanhuma (Exodus, Piqudei 3), which describes the procedure through which God determines the characteristics of a person who is about to be conceived. God chooses whether the person will be male or female, strong or weak, and selects as well a range of other characteristics. But whether the individual will be wicked or righteous is left to the person's own free will. This aspect of the person's life, that is to say, is determined by the behaviors selected by the soul:

> A. Immediately, the Holy One, blessed be he, motions to the angel in charge of the souls (*ruachot*) and tells him, "Bring me this certain soul (*ruach*), which is in the Garden of Eden, whose name is Such-and-So, and whose appearance is such-and-such." For all of the souls (*ruachot*) that were ever to be created, all of them were created on the day that [God] created the world.
>
> B. Before the world will come to an end, they will be assigned to [specific] people, as it is written [Eccl 6:10]: "Whatever will come to be has already been named."
>
> C. Immediately, the angel goes and brings the soul (*ruach*) before the Holy One, blessed be he. And when that soul comes, immediately it bends down and bows its knees

before the King of kings of kings, the Holy One, blessed be he. At that time, the Holy One, blessed be he, says to that soul, "Enter into this drop [of semen] of So-and-So!"

D. The soul (*ruach*) opens its mouth and says to him: "Master of the universe! The world in which I have lived from the day on which you created me is good enough for me! Why do you wish to place me in that decaying drop, for I am holy and pure, and I have been hewn from your glory."

E. Immediately, the Holy One, blessed be he, says to this soul (*neshamah*), "The world into which I am going to place you is better for you than the one in which you have lived until now. And, at the time at which I created you, I created you only for this [particular] drop!"

F. Immediately, the Holy One, blessed be he, places it there against its will, and then the angel goes and places the soul (*ruach*) in the womb of its mother. And they call upon two [other] angels, which watch over it, so that it does not leave there and so that it does not miscarry.

G. And they place there a lit candle on its head, as Scripture states [Job 29:3], "Oh, that I were as in the months of old, as in the days when God watched over me; when his lamp shone upon my head [and by his light I walked through darkness]."

H. And [by that candle's light] it can look and see from one end of the world to the other. The angel takes it from there and brings it to the Garden of Eden, and shows it the righteous sitting in glory with their crowns on their heads, and the angel says to that soul (*ruach*), "Do you know who these are?"

I. Says to him the soul (*ruach*), "No, my lord."

J. So the angel continues and says, "They that you see were created in the beginning just like you, within the wombs of their mothers, and they went out into the world and observed the Torah and the commandments. Therefore, they were deemed worthy, and this good that you see came to them. Know that you are destined to leave the world [upon the death of the body into which you are placed], and if you are worthy and observe the Torah of the Holy One, blessed be he, you will be worthy of this and of the same place they [earned].

K. "But if not, know and realize that you will be worthy of a different place."

While created as a part of God, separately from the body that it will eventually animate, the soul has no meaningful existence outside of that body. It knows nothing of the world, which God, notably, tells the soul is a better place than the heavenly one in which the soul so far has abided (E). Once it is placed within the growing embryo, the soul is shown all of the world and made aware of its potential to do good or evil (H). Only in its bodily existence, this is to say, might the soul accomplish God's will for it, which is to follow the Torah and commandments. If it does this, it and the body will merit eternal life in the Garden of Eden, where the soul already has been shown the other "righteous" abiding in glory.

We see that, while the rabbis understand the soul to be a divine creation that preexists the body and is eternal, they hold that it has no meaningful existence outside of the body.[13] Further, even though the soul refers to itself as "holy and pure" (D), it is not in fact intrinsically good or bad. The soul and body, rather, are responsible for the choices they together make in their embodied form. The soul, therefore, as much as the body, ultimately will be judged for its actions within the body that was its home.

The rabbis' notion that the soul participates in, but does not entirely control, the choice of how the person lives his or her life is made clear at Babylonian Talmud Sanhedrin 91a–b. At the time of the resurrection, the soul and body will be brought back together for judgment.

A. Antoninus said to Rabbi [Judah the Patriarch],[14] "The body and the soul (*neshamah*) both can exempt themselves from judgment. How so? The body will say, 'The soul is the one that has sinned, for from the day that it left me, lo, I am left like a silent stone in the grave.' And the soul will say, 'The body is the one that sinned. For from the day that I left it, lo, I have been flying about in the air like a bird.'"

B. [Judah] said to him, "I shall draw a parable for you. To what may the matter be likened? To the case of a mortal king who had a lovely orchard, and in it were [91b] luscious figs. He set in it two watchmen, one crippled and one blind. Said the cripple to the blind man, 'There are luscious figs that I see in the orchard. Come and carry me, and let us get some to eat. The cripple rode on the blind man and they got the figs and ate them. After a while the king said to them, 'Where are the luscious figs?'

C. "Said the cripple, 'Do I have feet to go to them?' Said the blind man, 'Do I have eyes to see?' What did the king do? He had the cripple climb onto the blind man, and he inflicted judgment on them as one.

D. "So the Holy One, blessed be he, brings the soul and places it back in the body and judges them as one, as it is said, 'He shall call to the heavens from above and to the earth, that he may judge his people' (Ps 50:4). 'He shall call to the heavens from above' – this is the soul. 'And to the earth, that he may judge his people' – this is the body."

---

13 Weiss, Daniel, "Embodied Cognition in Classical Rabbinic Literature," *Zygon: Journal of Religion and Science* 48–3 (2013), 796, puts the point as follows: ". . . there is no indication that the soul has any distinctive functions that could be separated from physical embodiment. There is no metaphysical opposition between body and soul, but rather an active functional unity: the soul's function is to provide animation and dynamic movement to what would otherwise be static and lifeless bodily components." Weiss overall argues that the rabbinic view, just like that of Scripture, is not dualistic at all. This is despite the fact that, in the rabbinic view, the soul survives death.

14 A number of Talmudic passages describe interactions between Antoninus and Judah. Scholars have asserted that Antoninus is either the emperor Antoninus Alexander Severus or Antoninus Marcus Aurelius (see Jastrow, *Dictionary*, 83). But an exact identification remains unclear. One problem is that the Talmudic sources refer to more than one Antoninus, an Antoninus senior and an Antoninus junior. Additionally, while scholars have suggested an early dating for these tales, they appear exclusively in the much later Talmud. This makes it hard to be certain of their early provenance. For an overview of the issues, see Gutmann, Joshua, "Antoninus Pius; in the Talmud and Aggadah," in: *Encyclopedia Judaica*, 2nd ed., vol. 2, Detroit: Macmillan, 2007, 248–249.

The question of the soul's purity[15] here finds a rather direct answer: neither the soul nor the body can sin without the other; each is equally subject to and responsible for sin. This means that, whatever the significance of the soul as the divinely created aspect of human beings, it has no intrinsic quality of goodness; it therefore should not be valorized over the body. Additionally, while this passage introduces an interest in the nature of God's eventual judgment, it leaves open the question of what happens to the soul or body after that judgment. The passage may presume that, while the body is destined for disintegration, the soul is immortal. Or, as in the preceding passage that depicts the righteous in the Garden of Eden, it might imagine the body/soul combination in some form retained in the post-judgment period, as indicated by that previous passage's reference to "the righteous sitting in glory with their crowns on their heads." Overall, even as this passage depicts God's judging body and soul together, what this actually says about resurrection and post-mortem existence is left open.

In this regard, it is clear that the Talmudic sources with which we are dealing do not address their subject with anything approaching a systematic ideology. Thus Babylonian Talmud Shabbat 152b, to which we now turn, is consistent with the previously cited passages' idea that the soul, as much as the body, has the potential for piety or sinfulness. But in this passage, upon death, the soul itself, separate from the body, takes its place either in the Garden of Eden or Gehenna, depending on whether, during life, it had been wicked or righteous:[16]

A. It has been taught on Tannaitic[17] authority: R. Eliezer says, "The souls (*neshamah*) of the righteous are hidden away under the throne of glory, for it is written: 'Yet the soul of my lord shall be bound up in the bundle of life with the Lord your God' (1 Sam 25:29). And those of the wicked are kept in prison. One angel stands at one end of the world, and another angel stands at the other end of the world, and they sling these souls from one to the other, for it is written: 'But the souls of your enemies, them shall he sling out, as from the hollow of a sling' (1 Sam 25:29)."[18]

B. Said Rabbah to R. Nahman, "So what about the middling ones?"

---

15 This concern is familiar from Jewish sources such as Philo. See Klawans, Jonathan, *Impurity and Sin in Ancient Judaism*, New York: Oxford University Press, 2000, 64–66.

16 The Talmudic passage that precedes this one in Tractate Shabbat similarly makes the point that evil people are evil in body and soul, and good people are good in both body and soul. Both aspects of the latter are rewarded, and, of the former, punished.

17 Referring to a teaching attributed to rabbis, called Tannaim, who lived in the period of the Mishnah, that is, through the end of the 2nd century C.E.

18 In its biblical context, the citation from 1 Samuel is a statement of Abigail to Kind David, expressing certainty that God will protect David from evil.

C. He said to him, "If I'd died, I couldn't have told you this fact: this is what Samuel said, 'These and those [the souls of the middling and of the wicked] are handed over to Dumah.[19] These get rest, those get no rest."

While the soul is immortal and a creation of God, neither its character nor its destiny is predetermined. The soul, like the body that contains it, freely lives the life that it chooses, of piety or of sin. The character of that life, and that alone, determines the soul's fate, which might be one of glory or horror. The soul, like the body, is punished or rewarded in accordance with its behavior in life.

At the end of our selection of relevant texts, it is worth considering the elegy *El Malé Rahamim*, which in Jewish liturgical practice is chanted at funerals and on memorial occasions. This text originated in Europe in the period of the Crusades, so that its origins are beyond the period in which we are here directly interested. At the same time, the passage fully encompasses the rabbinic conception we have detailed of a reified soul that, while divine in origin and immortal, also is firmly connected to the body that it inhabited:

> O God, full of compassion, exalted in the heights, grant perfect rest under the wings of the Shekhina, among the holy and pure, who shine like the glow of the firmament, to the soul (*neshamah*) of the deceased, who has gone to his eternal home. May the Garden of Eden be his resting place. Master of mercy, we beseech you, shelter him eternally in the shelter of your wings. May his soul (*neshamah*) be bound up in the bond of life. The Lord is his portion. May he rest on his bier in peace. And let us say, Amen.

Here the concept of the soul is tightly connected to thinking about resurrection, which for the rabbis is always bodily. Thus we find imagery taken from 1 Samuel regarding the souls of the righteous being hidden away under God's throne. The passage further evokes the biblical book of Daniel's image of the dead shining with the brightness of the heavens (Daniel 12:1–4). And, finally, as we have seen in previous sources, the garden of Eden, humanity's first home, will also be its final place.[20]

As in the passages reviewed above, the rabbis here portray an eschatological image involving the corruptible body and an immortal soul. At the same time, their view of the soul and of the afterlife is neither well developed nor cogent. In the *El Malé Rahamim*, the souls (and/or bodies) of the dead shine in the heavens, reside in Eden, and are found under the wings of the manifestation of God known as the Shekhina; and yet, at the same time, the bodies – and perhaps souls as well? – find peace in the grave. Thus in the liturgy's focus on death and the soul,

19 That is, the divine being who in the rabbinic literature has authority over the wicked dead.
20 Cf. Segal, *Life after Death*, 622–623.

as in the selection of rabbinic passages we have reviewed, the picture is more evocative than it is cogent.

3 The Soul in Medieval and Modern Judaism

The rabbinic materials we have reviewed depict a close and elemental connection between body and soul. The implication is that the soul, while more clearly distinguished from the body than it is in the Hebrew Bible, remains for the rabbis of secondary concern and importance in their consideration both of what a person's focus should be on earth and on expectations for an afterlife. For the rabbis, this is to say, the afterlife is bodily. But even as the Talmudic rabbis developed this distinctive viewpoint, which became central in most future forms of Judaism, by medieval times, a Platonic perspective – focused on the distinction between the corruptible body and the immortal and incorporeal soul – also found its place in Judaism. This was the case beginning with the first century C.E. Alexandrian Jewish philosopher Philo[21] and continuing throughout medieval Jewish theology in the orbit of Islam.[22] Such Platonic thinking is perhaps most clearly represented by Isaac Israeli (832–932 C.E.; Egypt and Tunisia), who phrased as follows the Platonic idea of the continued life of the soul after the death of the body:[23]

> He becomes spiritual and will be joined in union to the light which is created, without mediator, by the power of God, and will become one that exalts and praises the Creator forever and in all eternity. This then will be his paradise and the fullness of his reward and the bliss of his rest, his perfect rank and unsullied beauty.

---

21 See Zeller, D., "The Life and Death of the Soul in Philo of Alexandria: The Use and Origin of a Metaphor," *The Studia Philonica Annual* 7 (1995), 19–55, and Burnett, F.W., "Philo on Immortality: A Thematic Study of Philo's Concept of Palingenesia," *The Catholic Biblical Quarterly* 46, 3 (1984), 447–470.

22 See Hughes, Aaron, "The Soul in Jewish Neoplatonism: A Case Study of Abraham Ibn Ezra and Judah Halevi," in: Maha Elkaisy-Friemuth / John M. Dillon (eds.), *The Afterlife of the Platonic Soul: Reflections of Platonic Psychology in the Monotheistic Religions*, Leiden: Brill, 2009, 143–161, and, more generally, Bookstaber, P.D., *The Idea of Development of the Soul in Medieval Jewish Philosophy*, Philadelphia: M. Jacobs, 1950; Reprint: Kessinger Publishing, 2006.

23 *Book of Definitions*, in: Altman, A. / Stern, S.M., *Isaac Israeli: A Neoplatonic Philosopher of the Early Tenth Century*, Reprint: Chicago: University of Chicago Press, 2009, 25–26, cited by Pines, Shlomo, "Soul, Immortality of. In Medieval Jewish Philosophy," in *Encyclopedia Judaica*, 2nd ed., vol. 19, Detroit: Macmillan, 2007, 36.

Similar thinking appears in a range of medieval Jewish philosophers, who argue, to quote Judah Halevi, that Judaism is "the religion which insures the immortality of the soul after the demise of the body."[24]

Medieval Jewish philosophers developed an understanding of the soul that emerged from the Platonic thought current in the Islamic philosophical context in which they lived. At the same time, these Jewish thinkers were in some regard constrained by the heritage of the Hebrew Bible, in which, as noted above, the dualism posited by Platonic thinking is all but absent. Given Judaism's biblical heritage, even as Platonic approaches to the soul are common in medieval Jewish thought, the opposing attitude of Aristotelianism also found its place. This is clear in the writings of Moses Maimonides (1138–1204, Spain and Egypt), generally considered the greatest of medieval Jewish thinkers. Maimonides[25] denied the existence of an immortal soul, particular to the individual, that lives on after death. He held that, after death, all that remains is intellect, which is not individual and the nature of the existence of which the Jewish philosophers who followed this thinking found to be largely undefinable.

Only in the medieval Jewish mystical tradition (Kabbalah) does an unabashed certainty about the soul's immortality and meaningful existence apart from the body emerge as an undisputed and central precept.[26] Within Kabbalistic thinking, upon death, the soul ascends through different levels of paradise (earthly, then heavenly) up to the highest spiritual world from which the soul originated. Even as the souls of the righteous thus return to and exist alongside their creator, the souls of sinners – which, like righteous souls, are immortal – suffer punishment, with possibilities including existence in a hell-like Gehenna and reincarnation. Through these processes the soul's deficiencies are corrected and a future existence in paradise made possible.

Within these new ideas, we see that both the unclarity and diversity of Jewish thinking about the soul found in the rabbinic period largely continued in medieval times. In this regard, notable, first, is the extent to which Jewish thinking tracks philosophical developments and ideas current in the world in which the Jewish thinkers themselves lived. Judaism, as we have seen throughout, offers no singular nor integral perspective on the soul; diverse ideas emerge as

---

24 *Kuzari* 1:103, cited in Pines, "Soul, Immortaliy of," 37.

25 *Guide of the Perplexed* 1:72, 74.

26 On body and soul in Kabbalah, see Fine, Lawrence, "Purifying the Body in the Name of the Soul: The Problem of the Body in Sixteenth-Century Kabbalah," in: H. Eilberg-Schwartz (ed.), *People of the Body: Jews and Judaism from an Embodied Perspective*, New York: State University of New York Press, 1992, 117–142, and, more generally, Ogren, B., *Renaissance and Rebirth: Reincarnation in Early Modern Italian Kabbalah*, Leiden: Brill, 2009.

are appropriate to each time and age. At the same time, second, we need to be clear that, within the mainstreams of Jewish thinking today, the rabbinic idea of a close association between body and soul, in which the soul does not entirely control the body and does not merit priority in our thinking about the value and purpose of human life, remains central. The previously cited memorial prayer *El Malé Rahamim* – unclear as it is about the nature and location of the soul following the death of the body – is emblematic. This elegy remains a central component of Jewish memorialization and hence of consideration of the soul in all forms of Judaism today. The approach found in the *El Malé Rahamim*, that is to say, is the construct through which the Talmudic rabbis' articulation of the concept of the soul ultimately enters subsequent forms of Judaism up into our own day.

4 Conclusions

Like rabbinic thought in general, the rabbis' thinking about the soul emerges piecemeal, in statements found in diverse documents and over a period of several hundred years. This characteristic – indeed, this limitation – of the Rabbinic literature gives us pause as we consider making a claim that on this or any topic the rabbis present a logically considered ideology. Still, the rabbis' specific choices in developing the understanding of the soul that I have outlined made very good sense within and helped to promote the larger framework of rabbinic thought. This suggests that, whether consciously or unconsciously, the rabbis reasoned quite purposefully as they developed their image of the soul.

These materials thus allow us to address the question we set out at the beginning: How do the rabbis develop Scripture's limited understanding of and interest in the soul so as to respond to the social and theological needs of their own lives and historical circumstance, circumstances, it bears noting, that were largely shared by Jews over the subsequent fifteen hundred years and more of Jewish history? In a period of Jewish powerlessness and loss of all that Scripture's covenantal idea had led Jews to expect, the rabbis needed to find a way to support belief in the existence of a divinely imposed order and meaning in the world. They needed to respond to an experienced reality that suggested either that the world was without meaning and justice or, perhaps worse, that the God of Israel had ceased to sustain and protect his people. The problem for the rabbis was to counter such thinking, to find God's presence and plan in a world devoid of any obvious signs of God's support for the beleaguered people of Israel.

In this context, the rabbinic approach to the soul was appropriate. If all souls that were ever meant to exist were created at the very beginning, then, however things might appear to us now, God in fact has a larger plan, a plan that will and must unfold in its own time and in the way God has already determined. The fulfillment of God's promises and the advent of God's kingdom, in however distant a future, were vouchsafed as part of God's plan from the time of creation. The fact that the covenant's promise – of the ingathering of Israel to the promised land – was not immediately fulfilled did not suggest that God had forsaken his people. God's plan was unfolding as God had established at creation. In the meantime, Jews needed to be, and had every reason to be, patient and to retain their faith.

In the context of this thinking, the rabbinic conception of a future judgment of reunited souls and bodies is important. It suggests that God's justice, though it might seem absent today, ultimately will be realized and will compensate for the suffering the pious now experience. The meritorious will be rewarded and the evil punished. This means that the world is not as broken as it appears. The suffering of the righteous and victories of the wicked will be made right. Most important, given the fact of a future judgment, acquiescence to rabbinic leadership and living according to the rabbis' rules matter in a way and at a level that people might otherwise deny. No matter how disordered the world appears today, learning words of Torah and adhering to Torah law exactly as the rabbis express them matters.

Within this context, the rabbinic view of the soul as, on the one side, connecting the person to the divine but, on the other, as consequential primarily in its existence in the human body made sense. In the rabbinic view, the body and soul depend on each other; neither, apart from the other, can fulfill God's will. This means that the human body, while earthly and corruptible, is a necessary part of God's plan. Our goal as humans must not be to escape or diminish our bodily existence. We need fully to live our lives and to achieve all that we can as embodied beings. Work, marriage, parenting children, participating in the life of the community are all central to what God intended for and expects of us. The presence in our bodies of a soul of divine origin that will live on past our death denotes our fundamental connection to God. But the existence of the soul does not change the centrality of the body in accomplishing God's will.

The rabbis' conception of the duality of body and soul thus supports the broad rabbinic ideology that focuses on the demands of life in the here and now, the demands of family and community. It supports the rabbinic program that directs us to worry about our life in this world and eschew the attitudes and practices, including martyrdom, that develop from an ideology that says that what really matters is spirit rather than flesh. An ideology of martyrdom and the desire to escape the body might have made sense in a world as broken as the one the rabbis confronted. But in the aftermath of the Jewish revolts against Rome that had led to so much destruction and death, and in the face of continuing Jewish powerlessness, the rabbis' assertion that body matters as much as soul was a significant declaration: for the rabbis, risking one's body in perilous military actions, on the theory that the survival of the soul would be enough, was not the way to accomplish God's will for the Jewish people.

Thus the rabbis insist that the soul, exactly like the body, can choose good or evil. This claim supports the most central conception of rabbinic Judaism: what we do, how we behave, our attitudes and actions – all of these are choices we have to make, body and soul working together to choose what is right. Since the body is not evil nor the soul automatically good, denying the body or blaming it for the ills we suffer is unreasonable. Nor is the attempt to remove ourselves from the community in the interests of becoming more soul-like, and so closer to God, an appropriate path. The soul, as much as the body, has its job to do in this world, and that is a job defined by the rabbis in their demarcation of what it means to live a proper life under the law.

To assure the Jewish people of God's justice and that there is every reason to hope for a future, perfected world, the rabbis develop the idea that each of us embodies an immortal soul. And they argue that proper behavior on earth matters exactly because it assures for that soul, and eventually for the resurrected body, an eternity of glory. This means that the rabbinic conception of the soul contributes to the rabbis' distinctive program of law: Follow the lead of the rabbis and you will merit a future in the Garden of Eden, along with all the righteous, sitting in glory with their crowns on their heads. To get there and to avoid the alternative of Gehenna, body and soul must choose what is right. By accepting and following God's demands, as detailed by the rabbis, one assures that death will lead to a divine reward. But to make this happen, one must think primarily about the obligations of life in this world.[27]

In Rabbinic texts, the idea of the soul and of a world-to-come thus serve as much more than a way of explaining either the injustices of this world or the experienced bifurcation of ourselves into body and something that seems to exist beyond the body. For the rabbis, rather, these ideas offer clear proof that human life is meaningful. Why do these documents speak of an immortal soul and post-mortem experience at all? Even if, to the rabbis, what will happen after death remains mysterious, they offer the very powerful perspective that what we do on earth matters and that the end of life is not the end of everything.

27 See Avery-Peck, Alan J., "Death and Afterlife in the Early Rabbinic Sources: The Mishnah, Tosefta, and Early Midrash Compilations," in: J. Neusner / A.J. Avery-Peck (eds.), *Judaism in Late Antiquity. Volume Four. Special Topics: Death, Afterlife, Resurrection, and the World to Come,* Handbuch der Orientalistik, Leiden / Boston / Cologne: E.J. Brill, 2000, 243–266.

Bibliography

Altman, Alexander / Stern, Samuel M., *Isaac Israeli: A Neoplatonic Philosopher of the Early Tenth Century*, Reprint, Chicago: University of Chicago Press, 2009.

Avery-Peck, Alan J., "Death and Afterlife in the Early Rabbinic Sources: The Mishnah, Tosefta, and Early Midrash Compilations," in: Jacob Neusner / Alan J. Avery-Peck (eds.), *Judaism in Late Antiquity. Volume Four. Special Topics: Death, Afterlife, Resurrection, and the World to Come*, Handbuch der Orientalistik, Leiden / Boston / Cologne: E.J. Brill, 2000, 243–266.

Avery-Peck, Alan J., "Resurrection of the Body in Early Rabbinic Judaism," in: Tobias Nicklas / Friedrich Reiterer / Joseph Verheyden (eds.), *The Human Body in Death and Resurrection*, Berlin / New York: Walter De Gruyter, 2009, 243–266.

Avery-Peck, Alan J., "Soul in Judaism," in: Jacob Neusner / Alan J. Avery-Peck / W.S. Green (eds.), *The Encyclopaedia of Judaism*, 2nd edition, vol. 4, Leiden / Boston: Brill, 2005, 2495–2501.

Bookstaber, P.D., *The Idea of Development of the Soul in Medieval Jewish Philosophy*, Philadelphia: M. Jacobs, 1950; Reprint: Kessinger Publishing, 2006.

Burnett, F.W., "Philo on Immortality: A Thematic Study of Philo's Concept of Palingenesia," *The Catholic Biblical Quarterly* 46, 3 (1984), 447–470.

Elledge, C.D., "Future Resurrection of the Dead in Early Judaism: Social Dynamics, Contested Evidence," *Currents in Biblical Research* 9, 3 (June 2011), 394.

Fine, Lawrence, "Purifying the Body in the Name of the Soul: The Problem of the Body in Sixteenth-Century Kabbalah," in: Howard Eilberg-Schwartz (ed.), *People of the Body: Jews and Judaism from an Embodied Perspective*, New York: State University of New York Press, 1992, 117–142.

Finney, Mark T., *Resurrection, Hell and the Afterlife: Body and Soul in Antiquity, Judaism and Early Christianity*, New York: Routledge, 2016.

Goldenberg, Robert, *The Origins of Judaism: From Canaan to the Rise of Islam*, Cambridge: Cambridge University Press, 2007.

Gutmann, Joshua, "Antoninus Pius; in the Talmud and Aggadah," in: *Encyclopedia Judaica*, 2nd ed., vol. 2, Detroit: Macmillan, 2007, 248–249.

Hughes, Aaron, "The Soul in Jewish Neoplatonism: A Case Study of Abraham Ibn Ezra and Judah Halevi," in: Maha Elkaisy-Friemuth / John M. Dillon (eds.), *The Afterlife of the Platonic Soul: Reflections of Platonic Psychology in the Monotheistic Religions*, Leiden: Brill, 2009, 143–161.

Jastrow, Marcus, *Dictionary of the Targumim, Talmud Babli, Yerushalmi and Midrashic Literature*, reprint, New York: Judaica Press, 1971.

Klawans, Jonathan, *Impurity and Sin in Ancient Judaism*, New York: Oxford University Press, 2000.

Levenson, Jon D., *Resurrection and the Restoration of Israel: The Ultimate Victory of the God of Life*, New Haven: Yale University Press, 2008.

Ogren, B., *Renaissance and Rebirth: Reincarnation in Early Modern Italian Kabbalah*, Leiden: Brill, 2009.

Pines, Shlomo, "Soul, Immortality of. In Medieval Jewish Philosophy," in: *Encyclopedia Judaica*, 2nd ed., vol. 19, Detroit: Macmillan, 2007, 36.

Segal, Alan F., *Life after Death: The History of the Afterlife in Western Religion*, New York: Doubleday, 2004.

Steiner, Richard C., *Disembodied Souls: The Nefesh in Israel and Kindred Spirits in the Ancient Near East, with an Appendix on the Katumuwa Inscription*, Universidad Católica Argentina Centro de Estudios de Historia del Antiguo Oriente: SBL Press, 2015.

Stemberger, Günter, "The Formation of Rabbinic Judaism, 70–640 CE," in: Jacob Neusner / Alan Avery-Peck (eds.), *The Blackwell Companion to Judaism*, Malden / Oxford: Blackwell Publishing, 2003, 78–92.
Weiss, Daniel H., "Embodied Cognition in Classical Rabbinic Literature," *Zygon: Journal of Religion and Science* 48, 3 (1 Sept. 2013), 788–807.
Wright, Archie T., "Some Observations of Philo's "De Gigantibus" and Evil Spirits in Second Temple Judaism," *Journal for the Study of Judaism in the Persian, Hellenistic, and Roman Period* 4 (2005), 471–488.
Zeller, D., "The Life and Death of the Soul in Philo of Alexandria: The Use and Origin of a Metaphor," *The Studia Philonica Annual* 7 (1995), 19–55.

Suggestions for Further Reading

Burnett, Fred W., "Philo on Immortality: A Thematic Study of Philo's Concept of Palingenesia," *The Catholic Biblical Quarterly* 46, 13 (1984), 447–470.
Finney, Mark, *Resurrection, Hell and the Afterlife: Body and Soul in Antiquity, Judaism and Early Christianity*, New York: Routledge, 2018.
Raphael, Simcha Paull, *Jewish Views of the Afterlife*, Lanham: Rowman & Littlefield, 2019.
Setzer, Claudia, *Resurrection of the Body in Early Judaism and Early Christianity: Doctrine, Community, and Self-Definition*, Leiden: Brill, 2004.

Eberhard Schockenhoff

The Concept of Soul in Christianity

In contemporary theology, the concept of the soul is only marginal. It is by no means a central term in theological anthropology; rather, it is usually replaced by terms such as “human being”, “individual” or “person”. Where the word “soul”, however, still plays a role in the linguistic world of Christianity, it points to the basic religious question of human salvation. To this day, the religious support of people by the official representatives of the Church is called “Seelsorge” (cure of souls) in German. The German translation of the Latin *cura pastoralis*, thus, becomes a kind of collective term which summarises important aspects of the Church’s activities, such as the proclamation of the Gospel, the celebration of the liturgy, the administration of the sacraments, and the encouragement of spiritual comfort.

In patristic and medieval theology, however, the concept of the soul played an important role in the context of anthropology, Christology, soteriology, and eschatology. The belief in the existence of an immortal soul served as an important terminological bridge in order to mentally grasp the Christian hope of man’s perfection with God. Even if individual Church Fathers such as Origen (185–253/54) temporarily advocated the theory of the transmigration of souls, which was incompatible with Christianity *per se*, Christian theology rejected the Platonic idea of a liberation of the soul from the fetters of the material world of the body. Eternal life with God and, thus, the immortality of the soul is not understood as an inherent indestructible substance as in Platonic thought, but as a salvific gift from God, which also includes the resurrection of the body. As a useful working definition that can guide the search for the meaning of the term within Christian thought, the following paraphrase may be appropriate: “Soul, in the theological sense, is the uniform reason for life of the whole body-spiritual human being. The term soul is connected with the theological statement that the life of man as such ultimately comes from God and, therefore, belongs to God and is withdrawn from human control.”[1] The concept of the soul, therefore, in theological usage, rarely stands on its own; within the binomen, “body and soul”, or the discussion of the

---

1 Langemeyer, Georg, “Seele,” in: Wolfgang Beinert (ed.), *Lexikon der katholischen Dogmatik*, Freiburg i. Br.: Herder, 1991, 465.

Note: Eberhard Schockenhoff passed away unexpectedly in July 2020 after finishing this article. He is thus the sole author of the text. The present volume is dedicated to his memory. (The editors)

https://doi.org/10.1515/9783110748239-002

body-soul unity of man, it normally describes a pole of human existence that, in the existence of a concrete human being, does not exist without the existence of the other.

1 The Biblical Roots: Equivalents of the "Soul" in the Old Testament

In biblical thought, "soul" often means "life" or "living person". Only marginally, in the Book of Wisdom and in the late writings of the New Testament, can the Hellenistic usage of the word "soul" be proved, which is used to designate a partial quantity of man, namely his spirit or his reason, which is contrasted with his physical-material existence. Otherwise, the following applies to biblical usage: "*nefesh* denotes that which makes a body, whether animal or human, into a living being."[2]

According to the oldest account of creation in the Bible, Yahweh forms man from the soil of the ground, breathes his breath of life into him, and thereby makes him a living being related to God (cf. Gen 2:7). This creation myth, in which old aetiological narratives are handled, does not tell of a unique historical event at the beginning of human life, but of its lasting dependence on God's creative power. As the eternally living one, God is always the origin of human life. If, on the other hand, he deprives man of his breath of life, he falls back to the dust, like all creatures: "When you take away their breath, they die and return to their dust" (Ps 104:29). In the same way, the Book of Job describes how the life of the perishable man depends entirely on the living closeness of his Creator: "If he should set his heart to it and gather to himself his spirit and his breath, all flesh would perish together, and man would return to dust" (Job 34:14f.). Man is, thus, stretched out between two poles of his existence which determine his life: He is placed by God at the head of all creation and is, thus, "the creature preferred by God, a little God on earth"[3] – and at the same time a frail and mortal being who shares with all creatures the fate of fugaciousness.

The fact that man possesses his life only within a lasting relationship with God is the decisive intention behind the priestly writings of creation theology. It

2 Harder, Günther / Schnelle, Udo, "Seele," in: Lothar Coenen / Klaus Haacker (eds.), *Theologisches Begriffslexikon zum Neuen Testament*, vol. 2, Wuppertal: R. Brockhaus, 2000, 1617–1621, here: 1613.

3 Cf. Kaiser, Otto, *Der Gott des Alten Testaments: Wesen und Wirken*, Theologie des AT 2, Göttingen: Vandenhoeck & Ruprecht, 1998, 279ff.

replaces the archaic metaphor of the vital substance of the soil and God's breath of life with the idea of creation through God's sovereign Word, which interprets the creation of man as a divine appellation, as the opening of a life-giving dialogue between God and man. "Then God said, Let us make man in our image, after our likeness" (Gen 1:26). Since the time of the Church Fathers, exegetes have put a great deal of perspicacity into understanding the difference between the terms "image" (*demut; imago*) and "likeness" (*tselem; similitudo*) according to a two-step scheme of salvation history. The dispute as to whether the contrast between the unscathed likeness of the blessed human being and the disfigured godliness of the sinner is actually concealed within the biblical expressions, in the present exegesis, takes a back seat to a fundamental hermeneutical question. A sceptical variant of interpretation denies not only that Gen 1:26 can be regarded as individual biblical proof of a theological doctrine of man's likeness to God, but also that within the Old Testament a self-contained imago-dei anthropology is developed at all.

The very fact that such a fundamental statement about the image-like nature of man, apart from Ps 8 and a few other passages (Gen 5:1–3; 9:6; Wis 2:23; Sir 17:3), is not often found on the ground of the Old Testament, according to this view, opposes a systematic use of this text.[4] If, on the other hand, one reads this verse, which is preceded by its emphasis of Yahweh's self-determination, not as an isolated statement, but from the perspective of the theme's framework of Creation through the Word, the apex of its meaning shifts. From this perspective, an interpretation seems possible, which is closer to the later theological doctrine of man's likeness to God and can be regarded as its biblical foundation. The focus of the statement of Gen 1:26 is, thus, entirely on God's action, in which the being of man is primarily founded. According to this exegetical view, the focus of Gen 1:26 lies not on a special quality of man or a distinction of being which belongs to him in itself, but on the "making possible of an event between God and man", in which the creative origin of human life is founded.[5] The emphasised relationship of man to God links the biblical account of Creation with Psalm 9, which also focuses on man's close relationship with God: "This and only this constitutes his special dignity."[6]

4 Vollenweider, Samuel, "Der Menschgewordene als Ebenbild Gottes. Zum frühchristlichen Verständnis der Imago Dei," in: Hans-Peter Mathys (ed.), *Ebenbild Gottes – Herrscher über die Welt. Studien zu Würde und Auftrag des Menschen*, Neukirchen-Vluyn: Neukirchener Verlag, 1998, 123–146, here: 137: "Biblical statements do not allow to sketch an anthropology based on the concept of the likeness to God."

5 On this trend in more recent exegesis cf. Westermann, Claus, *Genesis*, vol. 1: *Genesis 1–11*, BKAT I/1, Neukirchen-Vluyn: Neukirchener Verlag, ^{2}1976, 214–217.

6 Irsigler, Hubert, "Die Frage nach dem Menschen in Ps 8. Zu Bedeutung und Horizont eines kontroversen Menschenbildes im Alten Testament," in: id., *Vom Adamssohn zum Immanuel*, St. Ottilien: EOS, 1997, 11.

According to this interpretation, the anthropological meaning of the biblical statement about man as an image of God can be clearly seen. In biblical thought, man is not called a being in the image of God because of his immortal soul, in which the spiritual faculties (reason, freedom, will) have their seat. Rather, the point of comparison lies in an early stage of the development of this idea, in the similarity of the outer form, so that man appears as "a reduced, three-dimensional copy of God and his heavenly servants, the angels."[7] Despite the ban on images, it was not unusual in Israel to speak of the figure of God; especially in the Psalms, human bodily concepts (hand, ears, eyes, arm, face, intestines, and womb) are attributed to God.[8] Similarly, statues of gods and sculptural or relief-like images of deities were widespread in Israel's environment. Such representational images aim to make the power of the deity visible by emphasising the similarity of the image with its model. However, a comparison with parallels from the ancient Orient, especially from the environment of Egyptian royal theology, which recognises the being an image of a god as an exclusive attribute of the pharaoh, shows where the actual *tertium comparationis* of the statement lies: in the kinship of the king or man with God and in the ability to rule which is founded upon this. The analogy between the king's supremacy in his political dominion and man's mission to cultivate the earth and care for creation is a considerable exegetical argument in favour of the classical interpretation of Gen 1:26 in Christian theology. This theology sees man's likeness to God as being rooted in the fact that he towers above all other creatures and can be God's representative and partner: because of his reason and his intellect.[9] The biblical meaning of the discourse regarding man's being an image of God can, therefore, be summarised by *Otto Kaiser* as follows: "Man being the image of God did not exclude similarities in form, but meant the kinship of the human spirit with the divine spirit, which enables him to subdue the earth as his living space and to rule over the animals, so that he can protect it from them and make them subservient to him."[10]

In addition to the creatureliness and man's likeness to God, biblical anthropology emphasises, above all, the body-soul unity of human life. In contrast to Greek thought, which sharply contrasts body and mind as opposite poles of human existence, the basic anthropological concepts of biblical language do not describe superimposed layers in man or constituent parts of his being. When

---

7 Kaiser, *Gott des Alten Testaments*, 304; for a closer exegetical explanation cf. Groß, Walter, "Die Gottebenbildlichkeit des Menschen im Kontext der Priesterschrift," *ThQ* 161 (1981), 244–265.

8 Cf. Janowski, Bernd, *Konfliktgespräche mit Gott. Eine Anthropologie der Psalmen*, Neukirchen-Vluyn: Neukirchener Verlag, 2003.

9 Cf. Thomas Aquinas, *Summa theologiae* I, 3,1.

10 Kaiser, *Gott des Alten Testaments*, 311f.; also cf. 308, where the author affirms that the Thomistic interpretation coincides with the biblical sense of Gen 1:26.

man is described as "soul", "spirit", "flesh", or "heart", the focus is rather on the whole of his existence, with different considerations. These terms are almost never opposed to each other; on the other hand, they are often parallel to each other, if simply the whole human being in the unity of his concrete existence is meant. Ps 63:1 says: "my soul thirsts for you; my flesh faints for you, as in a dry and weary land where there is no water." In Ps 84:2, three basic anthropological concepts appear in equal coordination: "My soul longs, yes, faints for the courts of the Lord; my heart and flesh sing for joy to the living God." In Prov 2:10f. the righteous are promised: "for wisdom will come into your heart, and knowledge will be pleasant to your soul; discretion will watch over you, understanding will guard you."

In exegetical literature this way of speaking is called *stereometric* or *perspective*. The Bible does not use clearly delimited terms to unambiguously define an anthropological fact, but rather words with similar meanings, which are put together according to the figure of a *parallelism membrorum* (= multipartite psalm verse). In this way, biblical language clarifies the essence of a thing by enumerating its individual aspects, which in the synthetic synopsis form a whole. Biblical thought and language, in contrast to the Greek, does not assume abstract concepts such as reason and spirit or freedom and responsibility, but starts with the limbs and organs of the human body in order to draw conclusions from their description to their function, which in turn reveals a certain characteristic of human existence.[11]

In the Old Testament, the human being is most frequently referred to as *nefesh*, which in modern Bible translations is usually translated as "soul" or the respective equivalents. The Septuagint, in 600 of 755 passages, translates this basic word of biblical anthropology with *psyché*, the Latin Bible correspondingly with *anima*. This statistical discrepancy shows that even the early translators noticed how inappropriate the Greek language is in some passages for rendering biblical thought.

This difficulty is exacerbated by the fact that some Old Testament linguistic strata apply the term *nefesh* only to humans or animals, while others use it for both. In the Yahwist creation story, for example, it is said that man became a "living *nefesh*" when God breathed his breath of life into him (Gen 2:7), whereas in the priestly creation story this word is reserved for animals in the meaning of

11 Also cf. van Meegen, Sven, *Alttestamentliche Ethik als Grundlage einer heutigen Lebensethik. Ein Beitrag zum interreligiösen Dialog*, Münster: LIT, 2005, 64f. and Brunn, Frank Martin, "Biblische Einsichten zur Leib-Seele-Thematik," in: Wilfried Härle (ed.), *Ethik im Kontinuum. Beiträge zur relationalen Erkenntnistheorie und Ontologie*, MThSt 97, Leipzig: Evangelische Verlagsanstalt, 2008, 69–95, esp. 70f. and 80f., which highlights the relational character of biblical anthropology.

"living creatures" (Gen 1:20ff.). Thus, the same word, albeit in the opposite way, serves not only to identify man in what he is in himself, but also to distinguish him from the animal.[12]

What is striking about the expression of Gen 2:7 is that man does not have a *nefesh*, but lives as *nefesh* and is *nefesh*. Often the term stands for man's desire or longing; in this sense it is used, above all, in the Psalms when it says that he "longs" and "hungers" and "thirsts" for God (cf. Ps 42:2; 63:2; 84:3; 119:20; 130:5; 143:6–8). However, the Hebrew word characterises man not only in his spiritual desire; it does not speak, like the Greek *psyché* of the kinship of the soul with the upper world or as, later, the Christian theologian, Augustine (354–430), of the longing of the human heart for the tranquillity of the divine vision. Hebrew thinking in its "psychophysical language" rather considers the human being from his elementary life functions and their organic prerequisites in order to associate certain characteristics of the soul with these body movements.[13] The basic meaning of *nefesh* is, therefore, breathing, on the one hand, and the throat and pharynx, on the other, whereby the original connection between organ and function still resonates clearly in the verbal character of the Hebrew nouns. From the first breath to the last, man is thought of as a living being that breathes in and out (cf. Jer 15:9), which in its need for air and oxygen is similar to animals (cf. Jer 2:24). The understanding of death in biblical anthropology is particularly revealing in this context: when a person dies, Yahweh takes away his *nefesh* (Jonah 4:3; 1 Kgs 19:4) or his *nefesh* "escapes" (Gen 35:18). The soul does not separate from its body, but the breath, and with it life, escapes. Where there is no more breath, there is no more life.

From this basic biological meaning, the word field expands to all human aspirations and desires. Just as elementary as his inhaling and exhaling, he experiences the desire for food and drink, for human relationships (cf. Gen 44:30; 1 Sam 18:1) and sexual companionship (cf. Gen 34:2). Furthermore, *nefesh* is the seat of individual moods and emotional life, which seizes a person when he is restless (Ps 42:6), despondent (Jonah 2:8), bitter (1 Sam 1:10) or cheerful (Ps 35:9). In legal terminology, the term also takes on the meaning of person or individual; in this sense, it is encountered above all in the talion definitions of the Levitical Holiness code (cf. Lev 17:10 or 24:17f.). In all these meanings, *nefesh*, however, refers to the human being as an individual, in so far as he is out for something and is shaped by his personal desires. The word, therefore, does not describe a constant being

---

12 Cf. Scharbert, Josef, *Fleisch, Geist und Seele im Pentateuch*, SBS 19, Stuttgart: Verlag Katholisches Bibelwerk, 1966, 68f. and Schmidt, Werner, "Anthropologische Begriffe im Alten Testament," *EvTh* 24 (1964), 375–388, esp. 379.
13 Cf. Kaiser, *Gott des Alten Testaments*, 278.

or a dormant quality of his existence, but rather the "entire uniqueness of every human being before God",[14] whereby the spectrum of his experience ranges from physical need to his personal mood to his spiritual desire. According to Kaiser, *nefesh* proves to be "the individual principle of life or self which makes the human being a person and determines his or her unmistakable character. (. . .) Thus, *nefesh* represents the whole human person in its body-soul unity existing until death under the aspect of its vitality. This is why the word can often be translated as *life*."[15] According to Schroer and Staubli, the *nefesh* represents "the centre of vitality, life force, and lust for life" in the biblical view of man.[16]

A second pair of words, whose scope of meaning partly overlaps with that of *nefesh* = soul, is *ruaḥ* and *leb*. The first word, if we translate it into English, gains its clear biblical contours only from the second. Spirit and heart together denote the vital personal centre of man, the seat of his feelings and passions, but also the place of will and decision, of rational opinion, and moral experience of conscience. In the translation of *ruaḥ* with *pneuma* or *spiritus*, on the other hand, the rational layer of meaning, which in biblical thought is more strongly connected with the concept of the heart, emerges one-sidedly. The *ruaḥ*, which varies in its genus, but is usually used in a feminine way when applied to the spirit-filled human being empowered by God,[17] originally also has a physical meaning; it refers to the wind and the moving air, from the fresh breeze at noon (cf. Gen 3:8) to the roar of the storm that makes the trees tremble (cf. Isa 7:2). As a powerful meteorological natural force, the *ruaḥ* remains under the control of Yahweh. As his creative breath, it stands at the very beginning of life (Gen 1:2: "And the Spirit of God was hovering over the face of the waters."), but as an instrument of divine wrath it also drives locusts, floods of water, or catastrophic droughts over the land (cf. Exod 10:13; 14:21; Ezek 13:13).

Applied to man, the *ruaḥ* denotes the creative life breath of God, who gives life to the bones covered with sinews, flesh, and skin (cf. the vision of Ezek 37:5f.), and at whose departure man returns to the soil (Ps 146:4). The breath is an indication of the vitality of man; depending on whether it rises or falls, whether it is pressed or slowly escapes from the throat, one can recognise the psychological

14 Seebaß, Horst, "Leben II. Altes Testament," in: *TRE*, vol. 20, Berlin / New York: Walter de Gruyter, 1990, 520–524, esp. 522; also cf. Schmidt, "Anthropologische Begriffe im Alten Testament," 381; Scharbert, *Fleisch, Geist und Seele im Pentateuch*, 62–64; Wolff, Hans Werner, *Anthropologie des Alten Testaments*, Gütersloh: Gütersloher Verlagshaus, 2002, 25–48 and Schroer, Silvia / Staubli, Thomas, *Die Körpersymbolik der Bibel*, Gütersloh: Gütersloher Verlagshaus, 2005, 45–54.

15 Kaiser, *Gott des Alten Testaments*, 293.

16 Schroer / Staubli, *Körpersymbolik*, 49.

17 Cf. the exact place references in Scharbert, *Fleisch, Geist und Seele im Alten Testament*, 19.

state of man, his strength or fear, his courage or timidity. Apart from this general meaning, which allows conclusions to be drawn about a person's mental experience and moods, *ruaḥ* also stands for the prophetic empowerment or the special charismatic gifts of individuals. Similarly, the power of the servant of the Lord and expected Messiah is based on the transmission of the *ruaḥ* of Yahweh (cf. Isa 11:2; 42:1; 61:1). Finally, the term stands for the eschatological outpouring of the Spirit of God. In this sense, it no longer means the special empowerment of individual charismatic figures, but the empowerment of the new man inspired by the Spirit of God: "I will pour out my Spirit on all flesh, and your sons and your daughters shall prophesy" (Joel 3:1; Acts 2:17–21). In this delimitation, too, the term refers to the empowerment of man on the part of God; it does not, like the Greek-Hellenistic concept of the soul, tell of the natural qualities of man, but of the divine power from which he receives his physical life and does good works.[18]

If biblical anthropology always has the whole human being in his body-soul unity in mind, the range of meanings of "soul" can only be grasped if the semantic investigation also takes into account the term which can be considered the most likely to be of a contrasting nature to *nefesh*. The fourth basic word of the biblical understanding of life is *basar*, flesh. A more detailed breakdown of the 273 references shows that this term, unlike those mentioned so far, which always express a relationship founded by God, and including man, is applied exclusively to humans and animals, but never to God. It refers to what humans and animals have in common, and in this sense means, above all, their physical life, which is permeated by blood. The collective term "all flesh" often stands for the whole of humanity (as in Deutero-Isaiah; cf. Isa 40:5f.; 49:26); but it can also include the totality of all living beings (cf. Gen 6:17; 9:16) or at least the community of people and animals (Num 18:15).

The *kol-basar* formula is integrated into a theological conception, in the context of the Flood narrative, by the priestly scripture, in which the later hamartiological and soteriological use of the term is laid out: All flesh is doomed to perdition because of its moral corruption, but God takes some humans and animals from the threatening judgement in place of all living things, and after the Flood, creates a new beginning again with all flesh. Because the covenant of Yahweh extends over all flesh, the flesh of man can become a symbolic sign of salvation. "So shall my covenant be in your flesh an everlasting covenant" (Gen 17:13). This enables priestly theology to give a new meaning to circumcision, which even on the grounds of the Old Testament could become a custom sanctified by tradition, yet be widely misunderstood. In the archaic symbol of loyalty to the covenant it no

---

18 Cf. esp. Wolff, *Anthropologie*, 63–67 and Kaiser, *Gott des Alten Testaments*, 296ff.

longer recognises an old rite of manhood or a purely hygienic measure, as later rationalising interpretations assume, but “a holy sign which makes the Israelite aware that he belongs to Yahweh, the God of the covenant, with his whole person, body and soul.”[19]

The term “flesh” refers to the human being as a communal being. In terms of what connects people with each other, the word is used in legal terminology to refer to family and clan relations. Applied to the individual human being, *basar* expresses the frailty, mortality, and perishableness of human life (cf. especially Job 10:4; 34:14). It does not only refer to the biological powerlessness of his creaturely existence, but also to the weakness of his will, which cannot follow the commandments of God. This ethical weakness of the flesh, however, is not connected with a dualistic devaluation that would exclude the frail, sin-prone human being from the sphere of life of the divine Spirit. In the eyes of God, human life remains lovable and worthy of divine affirmation even in its creaturely weakness. A word from wisdom literature, which has provided the title for an ecumenical memorandum of both Christian churches in Germany, explicitly emphasises God’s love for the life of his creatures, even where it is weak and miserable: “You love everything that is and detest nothing of what you have done; for if you had hated something, you would not have created it (. . .). You spare everything because it is your property, Lord, you friend of life” (Wis 11:24–26).

However, in the elapsing field of meaning of these anthropological terms, a common basic trait is always maintained, which distinguishes biblical thought from the conception of man in Greek philosophy. The basic words soul, spirit, heart, and flesh do not designate individual layers in man from which his existence is built or which, after they have fallen apart in the alienated state of his life, would have to be brought back into an original hierarchical order to one another. Rather, the biblical designations read from individual organs and biological life functions, reveal various possibilities of man, each of which is given to him with different consideration. They view the holistic reality of his existence from different sides and, thus, are able to see the human being equally in his neediness and frailty, in his creaturely longing and desire, in his social relation and his individuality. The life of man is always determined according to the relationship which relates to the creative life force of God. The contrast between “flesh”, on the one hand, and “spirit/soul”, on the other hand, does not express an anthropological contradiction in man, but rather a contradictory relationship of the creature to its Creator.[20]

---

19 Scharbert, *Fleisch, Geist und Seele im Alten Testament*, 50.

20 Cf. Schmidt, *Anthropologische Begriffe im Alten Testament*, 387 and Schroer / Staubli, *Körpersymbolik*, 161–169.

This resolute standpoint of unity forms the background against which the basic anthropological convictions of the apostle Paul later developed. His theological understanding of man reconciled with God through Christ is based on the premise that man is determined as a whole by grace or sin. In the reconciled human being, it is not a higher pneumatic substance or the indestructible core of his better self that emerges; rather, the justified human being, who is only flesh in himself, is under the influence of the Spirit, because God turns to him and gives him a share in the indestructible reality of his divine life. Man's being is, thus, always qualified by the relationship in which he concretely exists; he lives either *coram deo* or *coram seipso* (cf. Rom 14:6–8), in the spirit or in the flesh, as righteous or as sinner, in life or in death. In these alternative possibilities of existence, the Old Testament juxtaposition of flesh and spirit lives on.

In contrast to the anthropological dualism of Greek philosophy, spirit and flesh in Paul's work do not denote two layers in man that are in conflict with each other – a rational "upper" sphere and the "lower" layer of physical desires – but rather the whole man in different respects, provided that he is either oriented towards God or closed in on himself. The term "spirit" (*pneuma*) stands for the life-giving power of God, as opposed to the flesh (*sarx*), which has a broader range of meanings: On the line of the Old Testament *basar*, flesh can, first of all, designate the physicality of man and mean the "mode of being of earthly historical existence";[21] in contrast to the imperishable *pneuma* of God, *sarx*, thus, stands for the sphere of the earthly and ephemeral, which constitutes the living space of man. In addition, the word "flesh" also refers to the origin of sin, which is not only manifested in individual evil deeds of man, but also in an inverted self-relation. Man lives a "carnal" way of existence by being content with the superficial, transitory life and relying on his own strength. In this qualified theological language, spirit and flesh, thus, denote two alternative ways of existence, each of which encompasses the whole human being as a person.

In addition, Paul also knows the trichotomic formula used in antiquity, which describes man with the terms spirit (*pneuma*), soul (*psyché*), and body (*soma*). Thus, he concludes his first letter to the Thessalonians with the blessing formula: "Now may the God of peace himself sanctify you completely, and may your whole spirit and soul and body be kept blameless at the coming of our Lord Jesus Christ" (1 Thess 5:23). Of particular importance to Paul is the term *soma*, for which there is no direct equivalent in the Old Testament. Of all anthropological concepts,

21 Brunn, "Biblische Einsichten," 87.

soma is the most comprehensive term by which Paul characterises human existence as such. The Protestant exegete *Rudolf Bultmann* aptly summed up the somatic way of human existence in the formula: "Man *does* not have a *soma*, he is *soma*".[22] While "flesh" is consistently negatively connoted in Paul's work in the sense of weakness, transience, and sin, "body" describes, in a neutral way, the person's inescapable habitat, the place where the struggle between spirit and flesh takes place. In this sense, Paul can even describe the body as a "temple of the Holy Spirit" (1 Cor 6:19); likewise, he invites the baptised to glorify God in their bodies (cf. 1 Cor 6:20). Paul justifies the prohibition of fornication by pointing out that belonging to Christ also includes being a human body: "Do you not know that your bodies are members of Christ?" (1 Cor 6:15).[23] Sexuality is not about an external part, but about the whole human being as a person who, if he wants to belong to Christ, cannot exclude the body-sexual sphere of his existence from this fundamental bondage to the Lord. For: "The body (. . .) is for the Lord, and the Lord for the body" (1 Cor 6:13). With Paul we can almost speak of a special dignity of the human body, because in him the obedience of the Christian is carried out, in him he carries the dying of Jesus, so that the life of Jesus may be revealed in him (cf. 2 Cor 4:10).

Contrary to the term *sarx*, which stands for the sinful encapsulation of the ego, "body" refers to man's creative mode of existence, his bodily action, through which he responds to God's action and does his will. In Pauline thought, the body and the ego cannot be separated. Rather, the following applies: "The body is the life form of the I; the I exists bodily."[24] In this sense Paul also speaks of a "redemption of the body" (Rom 8:23), by which, in contrast to Gnostic ideas, he does not mean redemption *from* the body or *from* the conditions of corporeality, but rather redemption *of* the body together with the salvation of the whole person. As an interim conclusion, it can be said that Pauline anthropology, in contrast to widespread tendencies in the environment of the New Testament, does not know the duality of ego and body, soul and body, but, following the example of the Old Testament, represents a holistic conception of the body-soul unity of man, which is very close to contemporary phenomenology's concept of the body. The basic anthropological concepts of biblical thought name the great alternative in which

---

22 Bultmann, Rudolf, *Theologie des Neues Testaments*, Tübingen: Mohr, 1977, 195.

23 Cf. Reinmuth, Eckart, *Anthropologie im Neuen Testament*, Tübingen: Francke, 2006, 237ff.

24 Reinmuth, *Anthropologie*, 233; for the whole spectre of meaning of soma in contrast to sarx cf. Dunn, James D.G., *The Theology of Paul the Apostle*, Grand Rapids / Cambridge: Eerdmans, 1998, 55–61; 70–73.

a human being must constantly decide: whether he wants to live as flesh, trusting in his creative self-sufficiency, or as spirit, opening up to his Creator.[25]

The Old Testament's understanding of life is completely oriented towards the phenomenon of natural life. Man's life as a created being is received from God in its concrete experiential form as a healthy or sick, a strong or frail life, and it remains dependent on Yahweh's constant devotion: Man is God's preferred creature, but he owes his life to the participation in the divine life which is given to him for a time. The pious Israelite, who sees his life as a gift of God, focuses his gaze only on this earthly life, despite its transience. Compared to all other assets, life is considered to be his most important asset. Wisdom holds wealth and honour in her left hand, but in her right hand she offers him "long life" (cf. Prov 3:16). "All that man has, he will give for his life" (Job 2:4). Faithfulness to God's commandments bestows a long and happy life (cf. Gen 15:15); even if man knows that he has received life only for a limited time and that, in the face of God's eternity, his existence lasts only a brief moment, he hopes to die "old and full of life" after a fulfilled life (Gen 25:7–15; Lev 18:5; Deut 5:16; Job 42:17; Ps 21:5). For the Israelite, a fulfilled life blessed by God includes, above all, peace and prosperity, fertility of the land, health, and abundance of children. Such a life is almost synonymous with the word "happiness"; for the Psalms, health, well-being, and happiness are nothing more than the epitome of life.[26] "For you have delivered my soul from death, yes, my feet from falling, that I may walk before God in the light of life" (Ps 56:13).

It was only in the late period of Israel that man's hope was directed towards an indestructible, eternal life, and the post-mortem perpetuation of his communion with God. In view of the crisis experience, that living according to God's commandments does not always bring joy and happiness, the Old Testament faith recognises that actual life transcends the physical and earthly dimension. It consists in the union with God, which alone survives death and withstands all life-threatening forces. From this certainty, the psalmist can accept the transience of his earthly existence. "My flesh and my heart may fail, but God is the strength of my heart and my portion forever" (Ps 73:26). In the face of the living God, he realises: "Your steadfast love is better than life" (Ps 63:3). Life on earth is also more than mere existence; it is fulfilled only in alignment with God. The connection between the fullness of life and the living relationship with God, which already on

25 Cf. Schmithals, Walter, *Die theologische Anthropologie des Paulus*, Stuttgart: Kohlhammer, 1980, 64; 88f. and Conzelmann, Hans, *Grundriß der Theologie des Neuen Testaments*, Munich: Kaiser, 1967, 195–207.

26 Cf. Bultmann, Rudolf, "Der Lebensbegriff des NT," in: Gerhard Kittel (ed.), *Theologisches Wörterbuch zum Neuen Testament*, vol. 2, Stuttgart: W. Kohlhammer, 1935, 864.

Old Testament soil leads to an initial distinction between life and living, is also behind the story of Deut 8:3. Yahweh makes his people hunger and satiates them with manna, so that they recognise "that man does not live by bread alone, but man lives by every word that comes from the mouth of the Lord" (Deut 8:3). This certainty gives rise to the hope in the later layers of the Old Testament of overcoming the fate of death and of eternal, imperishable life with God (cf. 2 Macc 7:9–29; Dan 12:2; Wis 4:14). In this context, the Greek concept of the soul can also be used in the sense of an imperishable principle of life that continues beyond death. For example, in Wis 3:1,4, it says: "The souls of the righteous are in God's hand . . . their hope is full of immortality." In Hellenistically influenced wisdom literature, the concept of the soul can also be connected with man's being an image of God. The hope for a just distinction for "irreproachable souls" is justified in this way: "For God created man for immortality and made him the image of his own being" (Wis 2:23). In contrast, the Old Testament does not know a preexistence of the soul. Wis 8:19f., a passage that is understood by some exegetes in a platonic sense, only states that the wise man received an "unspoilt body" at conception because he was assigned a "good soul". That his soul already existed before the body was formed cannot be deduced from this idea.[27]

2 The Biblical Roots: The Use of *Psyché* in the New Testament

For the New Testament too, life is not a static concept of ownership, but a dynamic concept of relation. Life is an expression of the relationship with the living God, from whom all life comes (cf. Acts 17:25–28). God alone is the one true Living (Matt 16:16; 26:63; Rom 9:26); in the unarticulated use of the early Christian missionary terminology, this confession becomes a proper name which distinguishes the living God from the dead idols (cf. Acts 14:15).[28] God alone is the Lord over life and death (Matt 10:28); he creates life just as he can take it away (Rom 4:17). From him all life comes; he is judge over the living and dead (1 Tim 6:13; 1 Pet 4:5). Even if the New Testament focuses more on the future life as the eschatological salvation of Christians, it is aware of the uniqueness of earthly life. In Mark 8:37 our present life is described as a priceless good: "For what can a man give in return

27 Cf. van Imschoot, Paul, "Seele," in: Herbert Haag (ed.), *Bibellexikon*, Einsiedeln: Benziger, 1968, 1564–1568, esp. 1567.
28 Cf. Stenger, Wolfgang, "Die Gottesbezeichnung 'lebendiger Gott' im Neuen Testament," *TThZ* 87 (1978), 61–69.

for his life?" The fact that the Greek word for "life" in this place is *psyché* (Vulgate: *anima*) proves that the scope of meaning of the biblical term is wider than that of the German word "Seele" (soul) and must be rendered with "Leben" (life) in many places: "Psyche in the New Testament refers to the human being in his comprehensive vitality, in which he finds himself, which he can receive or lose, preserve or give away. By no means does psyche designate a higher part of the human being, and even an abstract definition of psyche is far from the NT."[29]

Especially the many healing miracles that Jesus works testify to a high estimation of earthly life. His messianic mission proves itself precisely in that he restores the wounded lives of suffering, physically or mentally ill people.[30] The power of Jesus is invoked to restore lost earthly life (cf. Luke 7:7, 15). The reign of God begins when the reign of life is re-established even in its visible experiential form. The healing miracles of Jesus are striking signs which ward off any danger of a spiritualisation of salvation: The strengthened relationship of the healed to God and their religious reintegration into the community of the living is experienced bodily in the restoration of physical mobility or the healing of a physical defect (leprosy, blindness). The new creation of man through the dawn of the kingdom of God, which symbolically occurred in the healing miracles of Jesus, becomes visible in everyday life through the restitution of the bodily integrity appropriate to creation.[31]

Thus, *psyché* is written in Luke 9:24; 12:20, and also in Acts 20:10, to denote the contrast between the living human being and physical death. The expression *pasa psyché* stands for the individual human being (Acts 2:43; Rom 2:9), but it can also be found in enumerations. For example, in Acts 2:43 it says: "And awe came upon every soul (*pasa psyché*)". The Greek equivalent for "every soul" can, therefore, also mean "everyone" or "all" in the simple numerical sense.

In a theologically more substantial sense, *psyché* stands for the process by which God and man come into communication. Fundamental to this use is the double commandment of love of God and love of the neighbour, with which Jesus takes up and combines two quotations from the Bible of Israel. In the first part it says: "You shall love the Lord your God with all your heart, with all your soul (*pasa psyché*) and with all your mind". Since the *psyché* is, thus, the place where

29 Schnelle, Udo, "Seele. III," in: Lothar Coenen / Klaus Haacker (eds.), Theologisches Begriffslexikon zum Neuen Testament, vol. 2, Wuppertal: R. Brockhaus, 2000, 1621–1626, here: 1621f.
30 Cf. Dschulnigg, Peter, *Das Markusevangelium*, ThKNT 2, Stuttgart: Kohlhammer, 2007, 40.
31 Kostka, Ulrike, *Der Mensch in Krankheit, Heilung und Gesundheit im Spiegel der modernen Medizin. Eine biblische und theologisch-ethische Reflexion*, Münster: LIT, 1999, 63ff. and Pfeiffer, Matthias, *Einweisung in das neue Sein. Neutestamentliche Erwägungen zur Grundlegung der Ethik*, Ber Th 119, Gütersloh: Gütersloher Verlagshaus, 2002, 64f.

man's relationship with God takes place, it – and, thus, the whole person – is saved (Jas 1:21; 1 Pet 1:9; Heb 10:39) and snatched from death (Jas 5:20). But it can also be handed over to destruction in the divine judgement: "And do not fear those who kill the body but cannot kill the soul. Rather fear him who can destroy both soul and body in hell" (Matt 10:28; cf. Matt 16:26 and Mark 8:35f.). This Jesus logion had a great influence in the history of Christian piety; it inspired the idea that "poor souls" are purified in purgatory to receive the final judgement of God at the Last Judgement.

In Paul, too, *psyché* refers to the whole of life (Rom 2:9: "There will be tribulation and distress for every human being [*pasan psychén anthropou*] who does evil") or all people (Rom 13:1: "Let every person [*pasa psyché*] be subject to the governing authorities"). In several places Paul uses the term *psyché* in the sense of "giving his life". For example, he is prepared to lay down his life for his congregation: "So I will very gladly spend for you everything I have and expend myself as well" (2 Cor 12:15 NIV); likewise Priska and Aquila risked their own lives for Paul (cf. Rom 16:4). The term *psychikos anthropos*, which stands for the earthly or natural man, reveals a typical Pauline coinage: "The natural person does not accept the things of the Spirit of God" (1 Cor 2:14). Finally, Paul uses the expression *mia psyché* in Phil 1:27 in the sense of "being in one accord", and the sense in which we (in German) still speak today of two people being "of one heart and one soul".

1 Thess 5:23 raises particular problems of interpretation: "Now may the God of peace himself sanctify you completely, and may your whole spirit and soul and body be kept blameless at the coming of our Lord Jesus Christ." According to the exegete, Udo Schnelle, there is no underlying conscious borrowing here from the trichotomic formula of Hellenistic anthropology, according to which man consists of the three components of body, soul, and spirit. Rather, Paul only emphasises that God's salvific work is for the whole human being: "What is actually new and decisive is the Spirit of God. In his use of *psyché*, Paul is in keeping with Old Testament tradition: Man is not the sum of his individual body parts; rather, the whole can be concentrated in one part."[32]

If we take a look at the manifold uses of *nefesh/pysché/soul* in the Old and New Testament, two complexes of meaning crystallize that became important for theological reflection. First, the Greek idea of a dualistic distinction between body and soul is foreign to biblical faith. In the anthropology of both testaments, the whole person is always in view, whereby the physical sphere is positively evaluated and the soul as the centre of the person is thought to be connected with the body to form a body-soul whole. Moreover, the life principle of this unity is not

---

32 Schnelle, "Seele. III," 1622.

an immaterial soul, but the Spirit of God, who as a creative force enables the believing human being to have eternal life beyond death. This is the second set of themes in which the concept of the soul challenges Christian theology. The biblical concept of resurrection presupposes that the continuation of human life after death is somehow conceivable. The Greek-Hellenistic idea of the immortality of the soul offers itself as a bridge of understanding for this, but it is in important points incompatible with the biblical hope of eternal life with God.

The belief in resurrection and the hope of immortality have something in common in that both include the idea of the continuation of life beyond death. There is, however, a great distance between the two motives in the way in which the togetherness of body, soul, and spirit is thought of in terms of the consummation of human life with God. While the philosophical conviction of the immortality of the soul is linked to an anthropological dualism that abandons the physical life of man to decay, the Christian hope for eternal life includes the resurrection of the body, because soul and body belong together, and both are embraced by the Spirit of God. Moreover, according to Christian hope, the post-mortem existence of man is not founded in an inherent incorruptibility of the soul as a spiritual substance, but in the creative power of God. "The soul as the self of man does not guarantee this last, new existence, but God takes it with him."[33]

However, the healing wonders of Jesus not only want to underline the importance of the salvation that can be experienced at present, but they also refer to the future life that will be given to mankind as a participation in the resurrection of Jesus. Amongst the synoptics, in Pauline and even more so in John's theology, life almost always means eternal life in communion with God, which now already grants people a share in the life of the Risen One. Earthly life is, thus, respected in its uniqueness and yet points beyond its intrinsic value. Because future life already influences the present and determines the actual reality of the faithful (cf. Rom 2:7; 6:11; 2 Cor 6:9), earthly life is not devalued. Rather, its unique value is affirmed by the promise that it will one day be totally destined to participate in divine life.[34]

---

33 Schnelle, "Seele. III," 1625.

34 Cf. Schelkle, Karl Hermann, *Theologie des Neuen Testaments*, vol. 3: *Ethos*, Düsseldorf: Patmos, 1970, 230–232.

3 Philosophical Reflection: The Soul as the Unifying Principle of Man and as the Organ of the World Encounter

In the history of philosophy, Plato and Aristotle stand for two opposite interpretations of the soul. What both have in common is that they understand the soul to be the spiritual principle of human knowledge. But the fact that the soul represents the spiritual in man already means the end of the similarities. This has to do with the fact that both think differently about the process of gaining knowledge. For Plato, the soul is ideational, because cognition, as a recollection of the archetypal ideas, happens through the soul, which saw it in its prenatal preexistence in the realm of ideas. For Aristotle, all cognition begins with the perception of sensory impressions, and, thus, in the turning to the material world. Accordingly, for him, the soul is the spiritual principle of man's life in so far as it helps him to achieve his holistic unity and serves him as the medium of the encounter with the world.

Since in contemporary philosophy, whose forms of thought are taken up by theological anthropology, what is meant by "soul" is dealt with under terms such as "conscious ego", "experienced self" or "person", the attempt to analyse the understanding of the soul must follow the debates that are conducted around these terms in contemporary philosophy. With regard to the concept of person, a similar difference, such as that which existed between Plato and Aristotle, is revealed with regard to the soul. A purely mentalist understanding of the person, as advocated in analytical philosophy following John Locke (1632–1704), seeks to link the identity of the person to the contents of his memory, to the continuity of the stream of consciousness, whereas 20th century phenomenological research chooses the experience of the soul-filled body as the inescapable starting point for the attempt to explain the spiritual acts of the person, his cognition, perception, and thinking.

3.1 Physicality and Personal Self-execution

A philosophical position that links being a person solely to the continuity of inner acts of consciousness and the ability to plan one's life with an eye towards future can explain why we associate the term "person" with the idea of an individual world of experience and a self-responsible life story. It is, thus, protected from a possible misunderstanding that sees in the person only one human body and one material object amongst others. In reality, however, this alleged advantage is little more than an intellectual Don Quixotism, for none of the serious concepts of the person succumbs to such a misunderstanding, least of all a metaphysical one, one of whose basic statements is the transcendence of the person in relation to the material world on account of his spiritual soul, the *anima rationalis*. The real question is, therefore, not whether personal identity is absorbed in physical continuity, but whether it can exist without it. Especially the fictitious thought experiments of body exchange between a king and a peasant, of surgical brain transplants or an electrical information transfer to several brains in different bodies, which, in this context, are often employed in Anglo-Saxon philosophy, show, however, that the assumption of a body-independent identity of a human person, which is only based on the claimed similarity of the contents of consciousness, cannot be maintained.[35] This suggests the conclusion that the bodily situation of our existence is not only crucial for the identity of sleeping persons, but also for the self-awareness of beings that are awake and for the recognition of other persons. Personal identity presupposes the body-soul unity of the human being, which cannot simply be understood as a parallel continuity of physical and psychological events. The fact that a person can maintain his diachronic identity is based on the fact that he is the bearer of all his life processes, both physical-vital and psycho-spiritual, in his body-soul unity. The question of where the soul is in a fictitious exchange of bodies makes no sense in a non-platonic tradition of philosophical thought, because the soul does not know an existence independent from the body.

Rather, the phenomenological research of our century has shown that every intentional experience of our consciousness is bound to an original body experience, which it calls the anthropological primal act of the "body". What this highlighted label means becomes clear when we relate the differentiation of "Körper" and "Leib" – which is possible in the German language and finds no equivalent in English – to the differentiation of "Me" and "Self", which is familiar from identity theory. While the dualistic assumptions of all varieties agree that they confront a mentally conceived ego as a centre of consciousness with a material body, the phenomenological view sees "Leib" as the medium of expression of our self, to which our highest spiritual acts also remain bound.

The semantic differentiation between "Körper" and "Leib" expresses an anthropological difference that can only be expressed in other languages by using explanatory adjectives. French phenomenology speaks of the "corps propre" or the "corps subjet" when referring to the "body" (in the sense of "Leib") of a

35 Cf. Williams, Bernard, "Personalität und Individuation," in: id., *Probleme des Selbst. Philosophische Aufsätze 1956–1972*, trans. J. Schulte, Stuttgart: Reclam, 1978, 7–36. On the possible objections to the idea that corporal continuity is a necessary condition to personality, cf. Williams, "Personalität," 37–46.

human being. These auxiliary terms refer to the important differences between "Körper" and "Leib": "Körper" refers to the objectifiable object of human existence, which is accessible to scientific explanation, whereas "Leib" refers to the subjective mode of existence of being in the world, which is experienced from the internal perspective of a conscious self. The German-speaking phenomenology, therefore, distinguishes between the "functioning" body, which is our body, and the body, which can mean any object and is, therefore, also called "corporeal thing" (E. Husserl). The analysis of the human experience of the body by Gabriel Marcel, who combines the distinction between physical body and body (as a person) with that between being and having, gained great influence: I *am* the body that I *have* as a physical body. An older use of language goes back to Aristotle: We only attribute a "Leib", i.e. a personal body, to living, animated beings, while "body" is also used to describe the inanimate objects of the outer world. In this respect, the semantic distinction does indeed have a certain tendency to devalue the body, which is reduced to pure materiality and mere existence.[36] Nevertheless, one can be in agreement with Bernhard Waldenfels, in that the possibility of linguistic differentiation reflects a virtually different aspect of human existence: "The terms 'Körper' and 'Leib' form a linguistic capital that should not simply be squandered by speaking of 'Körper' when referring to the 'Leib'."[37]

Our perception of the outside world is not only dependent on the physical sensory data we take in through our eyes, ears, and nose. It is even more originally characterised by a certain perspective, which is bound to the spatio-temporal being in the world of our body.[38] Likewise, our self-perception is inconceivable without the experience of our corporeality, just as, conversely, we do not have a pure body experience that is not accompanied, at the same time, by the qualities of experience of our self as conformity and joy, conflict or pain.[39] Even the perception of our own body cannot be achieved through a neutral self-attribution of external body features, which could be done from an uninvolved observer's point of view. Rather, it presupposes the original self-awareness of our conscious ego.

36 Cf. Ammicht-Quinn, Regina, *Körper – Religion – Sexualität. Theologische Reflexionen zur Ethik der Geschlechter*, Mainz: Matthias-Grünewald-Verlag, 1999, 31.

37 Waldenfels, Bernhard, *Das leibliche Selbst*, Frankfurt a. M.: Suhrkamp, ^{3}2006, 15. Cf. also Kather, Regine, *Person. Die Begründung menschlicher Identität*, Darmstadt: Wissenschaftliche Buchgesellschaft, 2007, 153ff.

38 Cf. Husserl, Edmund, *Cartesianische Meditationen. Die Krisis der europäischen Wissenschaften und die transzendentale Phänomenologie*, Gesammelte Schriften 8, Hamburg: Meiner, 1992, 119 and Schöpf, Alfred, "Das Leib-Seele-Problem in phänomenologischer Sicht," in: Karl-E. Bühler (ed.), *Aspekte des Leib-Seele-Problems. Philosophie, Medizin, Künstliche Intelligenz*, Würzburg: Königshausen und Naumann, 1980, esp. 197–199.

39 Cf. Hastedt, Heiner, *Das Leib-Seele-Problem*, Berlin: Suhrkamp, 1988, 226f.

A simple experiment can clarify the mutual connection between self-awareness and corporeality: In order to recognise our own body on a surface that reflects from all sides and to identify it as belonging to our ego, we must fall back on an "inner" self-awareness that does not again rest on external identification features. On the other hand, in all attempts to look at our own body, we presuppose its living gaze, so that even the attempted self-distance still takes place from a body-bound perspective. Being in the body remains the inescapable situation of our selfhood, which we cannot omit even in the attempt of our conscious self-identification "from the outside". If we want to express this connection with the concept of the soul, it is again confirmed: We cannot experience our soul through body-independent introspection, but only in how it shapes, moves, and keeps our body alive.

This physical situation, from which there is no turning back, also structures our perception of space and our perception of the world. In a homogeneous space there is no "above" and "below", no "front" and "back", but only mere expansion. Spatial differences between the objects of perception only arise due to the animated corporeality of the human being. This does not only denote a certain place in space, an arbitrary point in space next to others, but a "bodily here", which functions as the starting point of our perception of the world.[40] It is only the perspective of observation marked out by the body that allows the world of objects in their relative spatial relationships to emerge; the "from-here" of the body is "the zero point, so to speak, from which space opens up."[41] Just as the body is the centre of a particular perspective of the world, so it is also the starting point of every directed movement. In contrast to things in space, which are moved mechanically from the outside and must be directed towards a target, the body's own movement is self-acting: It is not something in space that is moved when I step to the door to open it, but through the body's own movement of walking, I allow the dead objects lying around in a space to turn it into a living space. All experience and all experiencing of our world happens from the perspective of the animated body; from the body-bound situation (from *situs* = location, place) of our self, our conscious perspective of perception is built up.

More so, all communication and all exchange among people develop "according to the guidelines of the body" (F. Nietzsche). In bodily gestures we express our attitude towards life and our feelings in happiness and unhappiness, joy and pain, health and illness. Our body is not only for ourselves the gateway to the world, through which we find entry into the rhythm of nature which welcomes us. On this physiological level, we humans only exist through a constant process

40 Waldenfels, *Das leibliche Selbst*, 115.
41 Waldenfels, *Das leibliche Selbst*, 123.

of exchange with nature surrounding us. Without food we cannot even live for three weeks, without liquid not even for three days, and without air to breathe not even for three minutes. However, our body does not only describe the assimilation process through which we transform a piece of the outer nature as nutrients into our own self.[42] It is also the medium of our self-expression towards the others, in which we make ourselves known to them; they have no other access to our "soul" than that which leads through the understanding of our bodily gestures, our laughter or crying, our cheerful and relaxed or our sad or tense facial features.

The term "body language" does not only mean a metaphorical way of speaking that supports the actual spoken and written language through physical gestures. Rather, body language – think of the reddening of the face of the angry person or the tender touch of the lovers – opens up a genuine sphere of expression, which often can only be put into words afterwards. This self-importance of body language is a consequence of the fact that we are not only through the spoken word, but already through our physicality, elementarily related to the communication with others. Waldenfels, therefore, speaks of the "body conversation" that takes place in our common existence: "To exist bodily means to exist in the view of others and at the grasp of others."[43] These have no access to us except the trace we offer them through the gestures of our life. Our inner world of thoughts, our feelings for them, and our own feelings only appear in physical form, conveyed to the outside world through our facial expressions and our entire posture.[44] When we write them a letter, they encounter our thoughts in the form of our handwriting, when we speak to them, in the spoken word, when we face them, in the impression we make on them through the language of our posture. The more intense our feelings for each other are, the more their urgency for the spontaneous representation in the body. The helping solidarity towards the suffering and

---

42 On the assimilation of food to our body and on the role of the stomach in this process Bachl, Gottfried, "Gedankengänge zur Leiblichkeit," in: Thomas Hoppe (ed.), *Körperlichkeit – Identität. Begegnung in Leiblichkeit*, Freiburg i.Ue.: Academic Press Fribourg, 2008, 143–161, esp. 144–152 has collected some inspiring stimuli from mythology, theology and ascetic piety, while philosophy nobly ignored the concrete materiality of food intake above its considerations of corporeality per se.

43 Waldenfels, *Das leibliche Selbst*, 240.

44 The function of the face as a revelation of the self and as a "window of the soul" was elaborated in a precise analysis by Plessner, Helmuth, "Lachen und Weinen. Eine Untersuchung der Grenzen menschlichen Verhaltens," in: id., *Ausdruck und menschliche Natur*, Gesammelte Schriften 7, Frankfurt a. M.: Suhrkamp, 1982, 201–388, esp. 250.

sick person or the sexual love of woman and man are inconceivable without their physical expressions.[45]

The reflection on the close interrelationship in which self-awareness and bodily experience in human existence stand in relation to each other, however, also shows an anthropological *difference* which is part of the experience of our body. We are connected to our body in all our expressions of life, and often, especially in physical emergencies and serious illness, we even experience ourselves as being painfully bound to it. But part of our bodily mediated self-relation is that we are not identical with our body. We are not simply at the mercy of its biological demands, but can enlist it for our conscious goals in life as long as we do not lose sight of its natural rhythms.

The relationship to our body is not a relationship of possession such as it is to the material things of our outer world. The relationship between the self and its body stands between having and being; the body that we are is not identical to the body that we have. From *Gabriel Marcel's* point of view, the paradox of man's body-bound mode of existence can be summed up in the formula: I am the body that I have as a body.[46] Helmuth Plessner, in order to express the interaction of the human person with his body, speaks of the "inward position of myself in my body" and of two different ways of existence, which he characterises with the terms "as a body" and "in the body": "Being and having constantly merge in the execution of existence, as they are intertwined. Sometimes the human person faces his body as an instrument, sometimes he coincides with it and is body."[47] In this case, being bound in the body is experienced as "imprisonment in one's own body."[48] Marcel even describes this reversal of the position of the human body as tyranny of the body, through which the priority of the ego over the body is transformed into becoming possessed by the body: "It seems to be part of the nature of my body or my instruments, in so far as I treat them as being possessed, to want to oppress me, me who possesses them."[49]

But how far does the leeway, which, according to our self-awareness in relation to our body, we have, extend? Is it only an unlimited plastic organ of expression for our self-representation as a person, the compliant instrument of our free

45 Cf. Schipperges, Heinrich / Pfeil, Hans, *Der menschliche Leib aus medizinischer und philosophischer Sicht*, Aschaffenburg: Pattloch, 1984, 13–33.

46 Cf. Marcel, Gabriel, "Sein, Haben, Hoffnung," in: id., *Hoffnung in einer zerbrochenen Welt? Vorlesungen und Aufsätze*, Werkauswahl 1, Paderborn: Schöningh 1992, 92ff. and Marcel, Gabriel, *Metaphysisches Tagebuch 1915–1945*, Werkauswahl 2, Paderborn: Schöningh, 1992, 108ff.

47 Plessner, "Lachen und Weinen," 239 and 373.

48 Plessner, "Lachen und Weinen," 245.

49 Marcel, "Sein, Haben, Hoffnung," 95.

will? Or does it possess its own language, in listening to which we are protected from neglecting ourselves in our personal existence? It is the task of medical ethics, in particular, to provide an answer to these questions with regard to concrete problems such as extracorporeal fertilisation, prenatal diagnostics, brain death, the perception of age-dementia patients, or medical decisions at the end of life. Reflection on the holistic status of the human person and the importance of his or her body-soul unity warns against underestimating the weight of the physicality of human existence in these problem areas. It is a momentous misunderstanding, in which many excesses of modern medicine find their cause, that we treat our body like an object precisely when we feel ill and miserable and perceive its burden as being particularly painful. The disregard of the mental experience of illness is a frequent cause of misguided decisions regarding treatment.

3.2 Physicality and Intersubjective Being with Others

The anthropological significance of our animated corporeality is finally revealed in the social dimension of our being together. We do not first experience ourselves as the centre of consciousness-experiences in order to then perceive ourselves in a social context in which we seek the encounter with the expressions of foreign states of consciousness. All human encounters take place in and through the body. When modern developmental psychology emphasises the necessity of intensive physical contact with the mother for the child's self-development, it is describing a general phenomenon that also applies outside the first phase of life. We never experience our own being as a self-contained, pure self-consciousness; rather, it only becomes accessible to us in being with the others, when we, in our physical counterpart, are with and there for each other. This is evident at all levels of human communication, when making eye contact and in conversation, in handshakes and hugs, and even in factual contact at work, where we react to the physical presence of others with instinctive sympathy or antipathy. Not only our language of sexual expression, but all forms of contact through which we come into contact with each other have a physical colouring. We can almost see in it an anthropological primordial date which can be expressed in the phenomenological principle: "Body and intersubjectivity are inseparably linked."[50]

50 Schöpf, "Das Leib-Seele-Problem in phänomenologischer Sicht," 202. Cf. also Wucherer-Huldenfeld, Augustinus K., "Das Miteinander als Zugang zum Leib-Seele-Problem," in: Günther Pöltner / Helmuth Vetter (eds.), *Leben zur Gänze. Das Leib-Seele-Problem*, Vienna-Munich: Herold, 1986, 27–48, esp. 34–36.

Our body is the interface of I and you, the line of contact of our individual selfhood with the world of others. There is no path that leads past our body to our fellow human beings or from them back to us; the others experience us only in our body, and we meet them only in their physical existence. We can, therefore, only respect each other by respecting each other in our physical existence. The freedom and dignity of the others does not only appear to us in their spiritual acts of consciousness or in the memories and plans for the future through which they open up to us. Our encounter with them is always determined by their physicality, even if we do not perceive them in immediate presence, but only as a voice through the telephone or as handwriting in a letter. We can, therefore, only respect ourselves in our personhood by acknowledging ourselves in the wholeness of our concrete existence.

3.3 The Hylomorphic Explanatory Model for Human Unity

After the previous philosophical considerations have shown phenomenologically how the reality of the soul expresses itself in its bodily expressions, the next step is to ask for a theoretical explanatory model that allows the workings of the soul to be understood as a unifying principle of man and as an organ of his encounter with the world. The most influential analysis of the body-soul unity of man, which is also compatible with modern emergence theories, which give a non-reductive explanation for the emergence of the mental condition, is the Aristotelian-Thomistic *hylomorphism*. It can be understood as an intermediate position between a naturalistic interpretation of the human being and the substance dualism of *René Descartes* (1596–1650), which avoids the one-sidedness and shortening of both extremes. Better than any alternative theory, *hylomorphism* is able to express the complexity of human existence from the physical-vital basic layer to the psycho-soul and spiritual and at the same time to hold on to the unity of the human being. According to the hylomorphic basic intuition, the spiritual soul (*anima rationalis*), which has both an animalistic and vegetative dimension, is regarded as the substantial form (*forma substantialis*) of an individual human being. It functions as the metaphysical working principle that makes someone the concrete person that he or she is.

According to an interpretation of the hylomorphic position that has been prevalent since the High Age of Scholasticism, the *forma* of a living being is to be understood as *actus primus*, i.e. as the realisation or the actual existence of an organism.[51] A living being differs from dead bodies and inanimate substances in that it has a soul as its principle of life. This not only brings about the unity of the organism through which this living being lives, but also enables it to carry out the characteristic activities of its kind. For the human being, this means that, due to the presence of his soul in his body, he actually lives and is capable of his body-soul existence. His organism is not only a particularly complexly structured body or, as in Descartes' dualism, a finely structured automaton, but the medium of expression of a person who represents himself *in* and *through* his body. Because the *anima rationalis* is the one principle of life and action of the whole human being, the pre-rational layers of the animalistic are also directed in a specifically human way toward its destiny of a spiritually shaped way of existence. According to the hylomorphic approach, the fact that man possesses a spiritual soul, by which he differs from other living beings who possess a specifically animalistic soul, means that he lives as a human being and is capable of performing typically human functions and activities.[52]

According to a common saying in the field of hylomorphic theory, man is a being composed of two parts, the body as the *materia* and the soul as the *forma*. According to this idea, matter and form are to be thought of as parts of a whole that exist separately and are only subsequently put together. In this way, however, the concrete unity of human life cannot be explained. For matter does not denote an independent part of man, but only the physical substrate *from which* he exists; likewise, the soul is not an independent part of the human way of existence or even the "actual" man, but it describes the actual being or being alive of man, who only exists in and through his body-soul unity. If *hylomorphism* is interpreted in this sense from the Aristotelian doctrine of act-potency, then the talk of man as a "composite" proves to be at least misunderstandable. It comes from the description of the process of how an artefact is produced. When a sculptor creates a statue out of wood or marble, this process can be interpreted in such a way that the finished statue is a whole composed of two elements, a new composite. One aspect, its *materia*, describes what it is made of, the other aspect, its *forma*, the new thing it has become through the activity of the artist. It is still made *of* wood, but it is no longer *just* wood, but has become a wooden statue or a statue made of wood.[53]

---

51 Cf. Gilson, Etienne, *Le Thomisme. Introduction à la Philosophie de Saint Thomas*, Paris: Vrin, [7]1979, 241f.

52 Cf. Runggaldier, Edmund, "Unsterblichkeitshoffnung und die hylemorphistische Einheit von Leib und Seele," in: Karl-Ludwig Koenen / Josef Schuster (eds.), *Seele oder Hirn? Vom Leben und Überleben der Personen nach dem Tod*, Münster: Aschendorff, 2012, 95–123, esp. 96.

53 On this example cf. Aristotle, *Metaphysics Z*, 1033a, 5ff.

However, if one transfers the manner of speaking from the partial aspects of an entity – which by their composition result in a new whole – to living beings, the unity of this living being threatens to be jeopardised. Admittedly, it is also possible to say in a meaningful way, with regard to a living being such as man, that the whole is more than the sum of its parts. Nevertheless, the soul in this whole must not be thought of as a further additional part, which would be added to the organs, bones, and nerve cells or – on a deeper biological level of description – to the muscle cells, blood cells, and brain cells. Therefore, the question in which organ area the soul can be located is also wrong. The soul is the life principle of the whole human being, which only exists in the interaction of all its parts, but not an additional part that would be added to the other organs in order to supplement their own functions (also possible without the soul) by another function – such as feeling, experiencing, wanting, or thinking – so that the human being becomes a complete whole.[54]

In fact, the body-soul unity of man must be thought more radically, i.e. already concerning the root and origin of the existence of a concrete human being. The human being as a whole exists as body and soul at the same time, not partly as body and partly as soul, but in the concretely permeated unity as this human being exists. He lives as this person as long as the unity of body and soul exists, and he ceases to exist as this person when the unity of body and soul has dissolved. There is no human body that exists only as a body and is not animated by a soul; likewise, in the earthly phase of man's existence there is no pure human soul that exists independently of a body which it animates and, thus, makes the body of a living human being.[55] If the body-soul unity of man is regarded as an expression of his being alive and, conversely, the breaking up into parts can no longer be regarded as life, then the talk of a dead human body or a human corpse is basically a wooden iron. To think of a human body that would not be animate and, therefore, alive is not possible within the hylomorphic frame of thought. Even in order to describe the process of decomposition of the corpse, one must still think of a somehow existing residual function of the soul in order to characterize the way of being of this dead organism.

54 Cf. Runggaldier, "Unsterblichkeitshoffnung," 97–101.

55 The problem of the *animae separatae*, the souls separated from their bodies and hoping for bodily resurrection, causes insolvable difficulties for scholastic theology. Thomas, however, accepts these difficulties when he maintains that the *anima separata* can no longer be called a human person (cf. Runggaldier, "Unsterblichkeitshoffnung," 107f.).

The material substrate of an entity is always only given in concrete reality as that in which this entity exists as living. Conversely, it is excluded that this entity could exist without its material "wherein" or "whence" of its existence. Thus, there can be no syllables without letters, no houses without stones, and no statues without wood or marble and accordingly, no living human being without bones, muscles, cells etc. *Edmund Runggaldier* sums up the strong concept of unity of man in the hylomorphic interpretation (if it is read from the perspective of the doctrine of act-potency) as follows: "Concrete things and individual living beings are units, but their *materia* is what they have become and what they now consist of, and their *forma* is what they have become and what they now actually are: Thus, Aristotle says concisely that *materia* (*hyle*) and *forma* (*morphé*) are one, one according to capacity (*dynamei*), the other according to reality (*energeia*)."[56] According to this understanding of the living unity of man, his being alive consists in his being one in body and soul and vice versa. Man lives in that his potential being actualises the material substrate from which he exists by the soul and realises as what he is: a living human being existing as a body-soul unity. The actualistic interpretation, which sees in the soul the life principle of the whole human being, is occasionally expressed in such a way that the soul creates a bodily field of expression for itself in the body or "achieves" its body.

This radical view of unity did not determine the Christian view of man from the beginning. Rather, for a long time it was influenced by the Platonic view according to which the soul uses the body like a tool.[57] The philosophical historian *Etienne Gilson* believes that all Christian theologians up to Thomas Aquinas held this Platonic view, handed down through Plotinus and Augustine: *Man is a soul that uses a body*.[58] Aquinas quotes the formula *homo . . . anima utens corpore* and ascribes it to Plato – in the knowledge that the latter stands for a different conception of man than himself.[59] Thomas sees the reason why their views diverge in the fact that Plato assigns feeling to the soul alone, whereas he – in accordance with the phenomenological research of the 20th century – regards feeling as an act of the whole human being in its body-soul unity. *Josef Pieper* sums up the view that first broke through in Aquinas with these words: "It is not the soul that makes use of the body, but the living unity of body and soul that is the real

56 Runggaldier, "Unsterblichkeitshoffnung," 101f.

57 Cf. Plato, *Alcibiades I* 129 e 11.

58 Gilson, Etienne, *History of Christian Philosophy in the Middle Ages*, London: Sheed and Ward, 1955, 361; cf. Gilson., *Le Thomisme*, 247.

59 Thomas Aquinas, *Summa theologiae* I 75,4.

human being. Not only the human being, that is, is essentially bodily, but the soul itself is bodily. It is its nature, it is soul by this very fact, that it is the inner form of a body: *anima forma corporis*."[60] Aquinas took this view in the assumption that only it corresponds to the Christian view of man, since any even latent devaluation of the bodily and physical sphere of man would be incompatible with the idea of his creation by God.

The Second Vatican Council expressed the strong unifying view of man, which is also the basis of biblical anthropology,[61] by means of a formula that deliberately avoids exact philosophical terminology. According to this formula man is *corpore et anima unus* (= one in body and soul). Thus, the basic intuition of the hylomorphistic interpretation, that the living human being exists only in his unity and that none of his different aspects can lead an independent partial existence as only physical, only mental, or only spiritual reality, has been preserved in its core, without adopting the special terminology of Aristotelian natural philosophy and metaphysics:

> Though made of body and soul, man is one. Through his bodily composition he gathers to himself the elements of the material world; thus they reach their crown through him, and through him raise their voice in free praise of the Creator. For this reason man is not allowed to despise his bodily life, rather he is obliged to regard his body as good and honorable since God has created it and will raise it up on the last day . . . . Now, man is not wrong when he regards himself as superior to bodily concerns, and as more than a speck of nature or a nameless constituent of the city of man. For by his interior qualities he outstrips the whole sum of mere things . . . . Thus, when he recognizes in himself a spiritual and immortal soul, he is not being mocked by a fantasy born only of physical or social influences, but is rather laying hold of the proper truth of the matter.[62]

60 Pieper, Josef, "Unsterblichkeit – eine nicht-christliche Vorstellung? Philosophische Bemerkungen zu einem kontroverstheologischen Thema (1959)," in: id., *Religionsphilosophische Schriften*, Werke in acht Bänden 7, ed. Berthold Wald, Hamburg: Meiner, 2000, 291–313, here: 305.
61 Cf. Wolff, *Anthropologie des Alten Testaments*, 25–67 and Janowski, Bernd, "Der Mensch im alten Israel. Grundfragen alttestamentlicher Anthropologie," *ZThK* 102 (2005), 173–175.
62 Text following the official English translation of Gaudium et spes 14, 1 and 2, online: https://www.vatican.va/archive/hist_councils/ii_vatican_council/documents/vat-ii_const_19651207_gaudium-et-spes_en.html [accessed 28.06.2022 by the editor].

4 Problem Areas in the History of Dogma: The Soul of Christ, the Doctrine of Two Natures and the *Anima Separata*

The fact that the concept of the soul in Christian theology serves to think of the body-soul unity of man in such a way that his belonging to the world of the spirit is not bought by devaluing his perishable body proves to be extremely momentous, not only in the field of anthropology. The decidedly unified thinking, which resists any splitting of man into a spiritual and material realm, leads to highly significant consequences in the field of Christological and eschatological constellations of problems. These cannot be explained in detail here, but can only be recalled in the manner of dogmatic-historical finger exercises.

4.1 The Soul of Christ and the Doctrine of Two Natures

The dispute over the soul of Christ accompanied early Church Christology from the beginning. *Origen*, the best-known follower of the thesis of the pre-existence of all souls, developed the idea that only the pre-existent soul of Jesus had always adhered to the divine Logos in undivided love and was, therefore, able to mediate between God and the flesh at the birth of the God-man – Origen uses the term *theanthropos* as the first Christian theologian. "None of the souls that descended into human bodies had a clear and authentic imprint of the archetype within them other than that of which the Saviour says (John 10:18): 'No one takes it [the soul] from me, but I lay it down of my own accord.'"[63] It is only because he has always been connected to the pre-existent soul of Jesus that the divine Logos, the eternal Son of God, can enter the body of Jesus. "This soul substance now mediates between God and the flesh because a connection between God and matter was not possible without mediation. Thus, as I said, the God-man was born, with that substance stepping into the centre."[64] The soul of Jesus is capable of this mediation, because it is not unnatural for it to accept a body and on the other hand, according to its nature as a reasonable substance, it could also accept God. In the birth of the God-man, the union of the divine nature with the human nature takes its beginning, "so that the human nature may become divine through close

---

63 Origen, *De principiis* II, 6,3, Herwig Görgemanns / Heinrich Karpp (eds.), Darmstadt: Wissenschaftliche Buchgesellschaft, 1976, 363.
64 Origen, *De principiis* II, 6,3; 363.

union with the divine itself, not only in Jesus, but also in all men who, at the same time, with faith, begin a life as Jesus taught, a life that leads all to friendship with God and to communion with him, who walk according to the commandments of Jesus."[65]

For Origen, the incarnation of the Logos leads to two natures in Christ: the deity of the Logos and the flesh of the humanity of Jesus. Nevertheless, Origen's idea of the God-man tends to be a biased one, which tends to see the meaning of the humanity of Jesus as only a temporary intermediate stage on the path of deifying all pre-existent souls. It is true that Origen expressly emphasises that the pre-existent soul of Jesus had "completely absorbed the Logos of God into its whole self and for its part had risen in its light and splendour."[66] However, for Origen, Christ's human nature is only of importance as a kind of initial spark that sets in motion the redemption process conceived as the deification of man. "With the resurrection, a process begins in which humanity is increasingly swallowed up in the divine."[67] Even if the later Origen did not pursue the audacious speculations about the pre-existence of souls in his exegetical works, they continued to have an effect in Alexandrian Christology for a long time.[68]

The history of the thesis of the pre-existence of the soul of Christ and its union with the divine Logos shaped the one pole of the early Church Christology, which is usually referred to in dogmatic historical accounts as the *Logos-Sarx* Scheme and contrasted with the *Logos-Anthropos* Scheme. The basic idea of the Alexandrian *Logos-Sarx*-Christology can be well observed in the most important orthodox representative of this school of thought, *Cyril of Alexandria* (d. 444). Whereas according to the Monophysite conception of *Apollinaris of Laodicea* (315–390), the divine Logos takes the place of the human soul of Jesus at the time of incarnation, so that he can speak of the "only incarnate nature of the God Logos", Cyril gives a different interpretation of this formula, whose origin probably remained unknown to him. He assumes a human soul of Christ capable of suffering, so that he can speak of two natures in Christ and grant the human nature of Christ its own principle of self-motion. Thus, although Cyril wishes to speak of two natures in Christ, he sticks to the unfortunate formula of the *one* nature of

65 Origen, *Contra Celsum* 3,28; cf. Gilg, Arnold, *Weg und Bedeutung der altkirchlichen Christologie*, Munich: Kaiser, 1966, 47.
66 Origen, *De principiis* II, 6,3; 363.
67 Gilg, *Weg und Bedeutung der altkirchlichen Christologie*, 47.
68 Cf. Gögler, Rolf, *Zur Theologie des biblischen Wortes bei Origenes*, Düsseldorf: Patmos, 1963, 230–260 and Schockenhoff, Eberhard, *Zum Fest der Freiheit. Theologie des christlichen Handelns bei Origenes*, Mainz: Matthias-Grünewald-Verlag, 1990, 208–224.

the Incarnate Son of God in order to make it clear that the Logos "did not appear *in* a man" but "became truly man, yet remained God."[69]

Cyril's adversary, the Antiochian theologian *Nestorius*, emphasised the significance of Christ's soul within the framework of a *Logos-Anthropos*-Christology, in which the unabbreviated significance of Jesus' humanity was emphasised by the fact that the divine Logos within the person of the incarnate Son of God in his human soul was opposed to a separate ego or person centre. As a result, although Nestorius was able to strongly emphasize the two natures in Christ, he could not think between them a hypostatic union (to use the formula which was later reached in Chalcedon), but only a volitional and moral union, which he called *henosis kath' eudokian*. In the eyes of Cyril, Nestorius, thus, leaves the ground of an orthodox Christology. He imputes to the Antiochene – as today's historiography of theology assumes, wrongly – that he is tearing apart the one Christ and advocates a separation Christology that can no longer think of the unity of the incarnate Son of God.[70] Cyril's own achievement is to be seen in the fact that he was able to overcome the weakness of the Alexandrian *Logos-Sarx*-Christology despite the retention of the ominous *mia-physis* formula. "The Cyril of the Nestorian controversy knows a true human psychology of Jesus Christ. Suffering, as in the body, so in the soul, and above all the importance of the human act of obedience and sacrifice is recognised in Jesus Christ. The soul of Christ has also become a theological dimension for the Alexandrians."[71]

The dispute in which Nestorius and Cyril ultimately talked past each other was based on the fact that in their theological disputes about the soul of Christ, they started out from an opposite understanding of salvation. Nestorius argued from the soteriological principle that the divine Logos could not have truly redeemed man if he had not accepted his humanity in its entirety, consisting of body *and* soul. According to the logic of this *quod non assumptum non redemptum* (= what is not assumed is not redeemed), without the acceptance of the human soul of Jesus, the process of God's incarnation would have come to a standstill halfway through, so that the very thing that was most in need of healing, the weakness of the human will, from which all disobedience and rebellion against God arises, would have remained unredeemed. The Alexandrian *Logos-Sarx*-Christology, on the other hand, follows an opposite logic: according to its underlying soteriological conception, the salvation wrought by the incarnate Son of God

---

69 Cyril of Alexandria, *Oratio ad Dominas* 31: ACO I 1,5, 73; cited in Grillmeier, Alois, *Jesus der Christus im Glauben der Kirche*, vol. 1: *Von der apostolischen Zeit bis zum Konzil von Chalzedon* (451), Freiburg i. Br.: Herder, 1979, 678.

70 Cf. Gilg, *Weg und Bedeutung der altkirchlichen Christologie*, 89.

71 Grillmeier, *Jesus der Christus im Glauben der Kirche*, 677.

would remain vague and uncertain, depending only on the human obedience of Christ's soul. Thus, Nestorius and Cyril inevitably had to talk past each other, even if both of them, within their respective frames of thought, combined the acceptance of Christ's soul with the interest of presenting the humanity of Jesus in an unabridged way. Since Cyril succeeds in doing this only in conceptual detours, whereas with his antipode, Nestorius, this has been the defining leitmotif of his thinking from the very beginning, the present research of Nestorius paints a friendlier picture of him than his opponent Cyril had painted of him.[72] The explosive effect of the explosives used in the controversy over the human soul of Christ is shown by the fact that for centuries Nestorius could not get rid of the suspicion of heresy that placed him at the side of the arch heretics *Arius* and *Pelagius*.[73]

4.2 The *Anima Separata* and the Intermediate State

The second dogmatic-historical complex of problems, in which the adoption of the Greek concept of the soul posed great challenges to Christian theology, is referred to by the keyword *anima separata* (= the soul separated from the body). In eschatology, this term is used to attempt to think of the status of man between his death and the eschatological resurrection of the dead as an intermediate state. If one combines the biblical conviction of the resurrection of the body with an interpretation of death, which sees in it the separation of soul and body, this leads to the idea that the soul finds heavenly bliss immediately after death, but still carries within it a moment of imperfection in that it still awaits the resurrection of its body. This conception, which was finally established by the constitution "Benedictus Deus" by Pope *Benedict XII* in 1336, is, however, associated with serious, basically insoluble ruptures and incongruities.[74] These are connected with the hylomorphic interpretation of the unity of man, according to which the soul is, by its very nature, both the whole form of the human body and a totally subsistent, indestructible spirit.

If one takes this radical anthropological concept of unity seriously, the interpretation of death as the separation of the soul from its body proves to be extraordinarily misunderstandable, at least if one wants to connect it with the biblical

72 Cf. Dünzl, Franz, *Geschichte des christologischen Dogmas in der Alten Kirche*, Freiburg i. Br.: Herder, 2019, 105 and Kany, Roland, "Christologie im antiken Christentum," in: Karlheinz Ruhstorfer (ed.), *Christologie*, Paderborn: Schöningh, 2018, 141–213, esp. 192f.

73 Cf. Hoping, Helmut, *Jesus aus Galiläa. Messias und Sohn Gottes*, Freiburg i. Br.: Herder, 2019, 200–205.

74 Cf. DH 1000.

hope of the bodily resurrection of man. For this attempt gives rise to a whole series of difficulties, which will be listed here following *Gisbert Greshake's* account.[75] *First*: If the soul is indestructible as a subsistent spiritual being, its continued existence after death can easily be explained. But how can the conviction of the immortality of the soul be reconciled with the idea that death really is destruction and the end of man? Doesn't this mean that a dualism is again being used to identify the "real" human being with the soul, which frees itself from its physical shell in death? There is a *second* difficulty associated with this: The remaining corpse, if one takes the thought seriously that only the living unity of body and soul can be called a human being or person, can no longer be considered a human body. The biblical idea that it somehow continues to exist separately from the indestructible soul, which already resides with God, and waits for reunification with it at the eschatological raising of the dead, cannot be expressed within the hylomorphic model of thought. Finally, a *third* conceptual incongruity lies in the fact that the soul also suffers a precarious loss of existence without union with its body. It continues to exist after separation from the body in death, but, if this metaphorical way of speaking is allowed, as a fragment and splinter. *Thomas Aquinas,* therefore, compares the status of the *anima separata* with that of a severed hand; moreover, on the ground of his anthropology, the soul waiting to be united with its body can no longer be called a person.[76] "For corporality is decisive for human personhood. Personhood – as the most perfect state of being – requires that the *anima* expresses itself in the body and is realised in *materia,* so that it can be *in communio* with everything through its body."[77]

If one takes the thought to its full-face value, that the human soul can only express itself in the body and represent itself in the world, one cannot avoid the consequence that not only the decomposing corpse but also the *anima separata* is in a somehow defective mode of being. The entire contradiction of this construction is further increased by the fact that, despite its unnatural separation from the body, it is already in a state of (albeit still diminished) bliss. These tensions and ambiguities, which Aquinas is unable to eliminate completely, basically stem from the Platonic remnants that overlay Aristotelian hylomorphism. The Protestant theologian, *Paul Althaus* (1888–1966), has, therefore, described the entire speculation about the intermediate state of man, taken over from late Judaism, as

---

75 Cf. Greshake, Gisbert / Kremer, Jakob, *Resurrectio mortuorum. Zum theologischen Verständnis der leiblichen Auferstehung*, Darmstadt: Wissenschaftliche Buchgesellschaft, 1986, 228–236.

76 Cf. Thomas Aquinas, *Summa theologiae* I 75,4 ad 2.

77 Greshake, *Ressurectio*, 229.

a "hiding place for Platonism", in which the dualism of Hellenistic thought could live on within Christian theology.[78]

Contemporary eschatology tries to escape the difficulties outlined by assuming a resurrection *in* death. According to it, the whole human being with soul and body finds its individual perfection with God in death, whereby the body does not only mean the material substrate of man, i.e. skin, bones, and tendons, but stands for the essential being of man in the world, which finds its end with death. Since the bodily existing human being is, at the same time, a relational being, the one and whole human being who resurrects to God in death must still wait for the completion of all, which can only happen at the end of times.

Both conceptions, that of the bliss of a bodiless soul as well as that of the perfection of the whole human being in death, thus, know a not-yet of this perfection, a waiting for the universal resurrection.[79] The representatives of the new model of thinking of a resurrection in death rightly claim for their approach that it does better justice to the biblical talk of the bodily resurrection of the dead and can avoid the incongruities inherent in the idea of a bodiless soul. Opponents of this concept – most prominently *Joseph Ratzinger* – argue that the distinction between the body as an expression of man's being in the world and the material elements of the human body also contains a latent dualism which spiritualises the hope for the resurrection of the body in a different way.[80]

4.3 The Immortality of the Soul as an Ecumenical Problem

In the 20th century, the use of the concept of the soul in eschatology is associated with a sharp ecumenical controversy, leading Protestant theologians to make a confessional distinction from the talk of the immortality of the soul, which most Catholic theologians want to maintain. In place of the portrayed attribution of the post-mortal existence of an immortal soul to the resurrection of the body, which is connected with a number of conceptual contradictions, the opposition between the biblical hope of resurrection and the Greek-Hellenistic assumption of an immortal soul is seen as a sign of recognition of the newer Protestant theology. In the history of theology, this is a contradiction to the philosophy of the Enlightenment, which – for example in the form of *Kant*'s postulate theory – wanted to hold on to the continuation of a rational core of human nature beyond death. The

78 Althaus, Paul, *Die letzten Dinge*, Gütersloh: Mohn, [10]1970, 155f.

79 Cf. Greshake, Gisbert, "Zwischenzustand," in: *LThK*, vol. 10, Freiburg i. Br.: Herder, [3]2001, 1530.

80 Cf. Ratzinger, Joseph, *Eschatologie – Tod und ewiges Leben*, Regensburg: Pustet, [2]1977, 148.

idealistic pathos of the ego, which, for philosophers such as *Kant* and *Fichte,* is combined with the philosophical rational belief in the immortality of the soul, is unacceptable to the representatives of dialectical theology (above all *Oscar Cullmann* [1902–1999], *Karl Barth* [1886–1968] and *Emil Brunner* [1889–1966]), above all because they suspect a titanic self-assertion of the human being against destruction by death. If the immortal soul is an indestructible core of being in man that belongs to his natural state of being, then according to this logic the claim to self-redemption must be hidden behind it, which Protestant theology can only oppose with an unconditional "no".[81]

The biblical statement of the resurrection of the dead, thus, becomes an absolute contradiction to the assumption of an immortal soul; it becomes a cipher for the radical powerlessness of the sinful human being who suffers a total *annihilatio* (= annihilation) in death. The traditional interpretation of death as the separation of the soul from its body is replaced by the hypothesis of so-called total death, which postulates an absolute hiatus between the earthly life of the sinner, who has fallen to death, and his new creation by God. But if there is no continuity whatsoever between the sinner's life on earth and the eternal life of the justified man with God, the identity between the old and the new man, which is presupposed in the biblical hope of the resurrection of the dead, becomes a problem. There is then no longer any point of connection for God's act of resurrection in the life of man on earth, which is to be saved for all eternity.

The fact that the same person, who suffers the total destruction of his earthly existence in death, is indeed saved by God then has nothing to do with the person itself, but is guaranteed solely by the faithfulness of God, which he shows to his creature beyond the abyss of death. On the other hand, there is nothing on the side of man that could survive death, no immortal soul and no yield of creaturely life destined for eternity to which the raising from the dead could refer. Rather, it must be conceived as a total recreation by God, in which the creature is completely passive and cannot in any way be thought of as a partner of God or as his created counterpart to whom he wishes to remain faithful.

This contrast also determines the interpretation of the resurrection of Jesus in the newer Protestant theology. If the Risen One reveals himself by his wounds and the disciples recognise him after the apparitions as the one with whom they ate and drank, this biblically attested identity of the Risen One with the Crucified One requires a theological reason. However, as *Jürgen Moltmann* points out in his

81 Cf. Greshake, Gisbert, "Das Verhältnis 'Unsterblichkeit der Seele' und 'Auferstehung des Leibes' in problemgeschichtlicher Sicht," in: id. / Gerhard Lohfink (eds.), *Naherwartung – Auferstehung – Unsterblichkeit,* QD 71, Freiburg i. Br.: Herder, 1975, 82–120, esp. 98ff.

"Theology of Hope", which was widely read in the 1960s and 1970s, this lies "not in the person of Jesus, but *extra se*, in the God who creates life and new being from nothing".[82] He postulates that Jesus can be identified by the disciples as the resurrected crucified one because of the resurrection by God. But this possibility is not only postulated as a completely miraculous event and in no way explained from the possibilities of the creative love of God, who holds on to his relationship with man beyond death. Of course, this presupposes that the act of creation is understood in such a way that God irrevocably places man as a counterpart endowed with freedom and responsibility in his own right. But if this is the will of the Creator, then there is no arbitrary self-sufficiency of man which he wanted to assert against God.

Rather, it must correspond to his being as a creature, which he has received from God, that man, as *Gisbert Greshake* remarks, in his being and doing inevitably stands before the living God. "This inescapability of being placed before God cannot be cancelled by death, but is finally confirmed in death as the moment of the final validation of the history of human freedom."[83] In this way he, at the same time, clarifies the meaning of what the immortality of the soul alone can mean in the context of Christian theology: "Human existence is from God, from creation, designed to stand before the living God for salvation or judgement and, therefore, to overcome the barrier of death."[84] The philosophical concept of "immortality of the soul", as it has been taken up in the Catholic tradition, does not want to express any claim to God by man who, in a titanic overestimation of himself, wanted to overcome the barrier of death of his own accord. On the contrary, the immortality that the human soul inheres by nature, as *Josef Pieper* has shown, must not be understood in the sense of an abstract metaphysics of essence, but only in such a way that it remains a gift of God.[85] "Precisely because of his concept of creation, which says that God, in creating, truly 'communicates' being, that is, does not keep it for himself, but gives it to *creatura*, so that *creatura* now possesses it as its real property – precisely because of this concept of creation, Thomas would insist that immortality is a quality inherent in the soul itself, founded in what the soul is by nature."[86] The philosophical category of the immortal soul, which is supposed to serve a theological understanding of the biblical hope of resurrection, is, thus, not only received in this process, but at the same

82 Moltmann, Jürgen, *Theologie der Hoffnung. Untersuchungen zur Begründung und zu den Konsequenzen einer christlichen Eschatologie*, Munich: Kaiser, ^{9}1973, 182.

83 Greshake, "Unsterblichkeit," 109.

84 Greshake, "Unsterblichkeit," 109.

85 Cf. Pieper, Josef, *Tod und Unsterblichkeit*, Munich: Kösel, 1968, 169ff.

86 Pieper, "Unsterblichkeit," 309.

time, changed in a decisive way. The legitimacy of resorting to Greek philosophy to explicate the biblical hope of resurrection then depends on how much weight is attached to both. This question, as well as the almost contradictory reference to the topos of the immortal soul, to this day, has been answered in different ways in the context of Protestant and Catholic theology.

5 Ethical Consequences of the Body-Soul Unity of Man

The Council's statement on the position of man in relation to the material world, to which he is bound through his body, emphasises his two-fold relation to the world: he transcends material things by virtue of his spirit and is, at the same time, immanent to their world through his body. He must, therefore, respect himself and all other people as beings of freedom and reason, without being allowed to devalue his physical life as something only material. This corresponds to the view of the biblical faith in creation, according to which man is both created in the image of God (cf. Gen 1:26) and formed from the soil (cf. Gen 2:7). As has been shown by previous discussions, this double polarity of human existence also corresponds to the basic assumptions of the phenomenologically oriented anthropology of the 20th century. What conclusions in the field of theoretical and practical ethics can be drawn from the bodily bound nature of the human being's reason and from the bodily form of existence of his spiritual soul?

In general, it can be said that the belief in the immortality of the soul in Judeo-Christian thought promoted and strengthened the belief in the unconditional value of every human life. Hence, the much quoted rabbinical aphorism: "Therefore Adam was created as the only one to teach you that anyone who destroys a soul is credited as if he had destroyed a whole world, and anyone who receives a soul is credited as if he had maintained a whole world."[87] This provoked, especially in Anglo-Saxon bioethics, the counter-question whether the conviction of the "sanctity of life" is not specifically due to religious attitudes, which cannot claim a general binding force in a modern, pluralistic, and secular society.[88] This objection must be countered, however, by the fact that the view of the

87 *Aboth Rabbi Nathan* 31, cited in Strack, Hermann L. / Billerbeck, Paul, *Das Evangelium nach Matthäus erläutert aus Talmud und Midrasch*, Kommentar zum Neuen Testament aus Talmud und Midrasch 1, Munich: C.H.Beck, 1922, 750.

88 Cf. Kuhse, Helga, *The Sanctity-of-Life-Doctrine in Medicine*, Oxford: Clarendon Press, 1987.

absolute value of every human being is not only based on religious roots, but is also philosophically founded.

The idea that free human beings respect each other in their moral subjectivity, only if they show such respect to each other in the manner of respect for the inviolability of their physical existence, has become increasingly prominent in the history of philosophy since the European Enlightenment. Even *Kant*, who at first could only think of man as a citizen of two worlds and who had to clearly separate his moral definition as a rational being from his belonging to nature, came to the insight in his *Opus Postumum* that we have always considered the corporeality of the moral subject in the concept of man. The organism of our soul-filled body now appears to him as the necessary outer space of our thinking, which opens up access to the world of others. Philosophical reason can no longer accept what it had become accustomed to since Descartes: that the body of man is pushed out of its self-experience and put on a par with the material things of the external world.[89] Rather, the human body, even after the modern turn to the subject standpoint of thinking, must be thought of as an expression of the soul, as a manifestation of subjectivity, as Kant attempts to do in the concept of the "necessary organs of reason" of cognition and action.[90]

Since the insight developed so far, according to which the personal dignity of man also includes the dimension of his physical existence, is often dismissed in the circle of Anglo-Saxon bioethics as a relic of the biblical view of man that does not fit into the philosophical tradition of modernity, this train of thought, which originated from the origins of the idealistic thought movement, is to be pursued a little further. In *J. G. Fichte*'s work, it leads to the conception of the body as a "fact of consciousness", through which the ego "forms" the medium of its encounter with the world and its effect on the material world.[91] The body is, thus, understood as an expression of the subjectivity of man, as its communication and visualisation in the physical world. The body is not yet associated with the notion of its given and often painful limitation or the recognition of the fundamental passivity of human existence. But on the ground of transcendental philosophy itself, the original idea of a pure, worldless ego has given way to the insight into the body-bound nature of all human existence.

89 Cf. Kutschmann, Werner, *Der Naturwissenschaftler und sein Körper*, Frankfurt a. M.: Suhrkamp, 1982, 252f.

90 Cf. Kaulbach, Friedrich, "Leib/Körper. II. Neuzeit," in: Joachim Ritter / Karlfried Gründer (eds.), HWPh, vol. 5, Basel / Stuttgart: Schwabe & Co., 1980, 180–182.

91 Fichte, Johann Gottlieb, "Die Thatsachen des Bewusstseyns," in: *Fichtes Werke*, vol. 2, ed. I. H. Fichte, Berlin: Veit, 1845/46 (Reprint Berlin, 1971), 596–609.

It is then *G.W.F. Hegel* who draws the necessary consequences in the field of practical ethics and philosophy of law from the insight into the pre-reflexive, bodily foundations of self-consciousness. Because the ego exists in the real world as nothing other than as a "body", the concrete "existence of freedom" appears in it, its necessary protective space in which it confronts the world of others. I myself can distance myself from my body, can try to impose the direction of my moral will on it and "take possession" of it in free self-appropriation. The people who confront me, however, cannot distinguish in this way between me and my body; for them I exist only in my body and am free only through it. "I can withdraw from my existence into myself and make it external, – keep the special sensation out of me and be free in the fetters. But this is *my* will, *for the other*, I am in my body". Therefore, in contrast to the restriction I myself impose on my own body, the strict principle applies to others: "Violence done to *my body* by others is violence done to *me*."[92]

Thus, the development of philosophical ethics and political philosophy in classical modernity also leads to the insight we have gained on the path of a phenomenological consideration of our self-awareness and our being together: Being in the body is the inescapable basic situation of our freedom, its concrete representation in a common world, so that we cannot express respect for our freedom among ourselves other than respect for our physical existence.

On the other hand, the attempt to isolate the biological and moral layers of meaning of the concept of person from each other leads to a shortening of our humanity that does not do justice to our self-awareness. If we base the morally binding core of the concept of the person on empirical evidence of formed personality features, we miss the claim of mutual recognition through which we perceive ourselves as persons.[93] In philosophical analysis we can distinguish between individual aspects of being a person, but these only form transitions of a continuum whose opposite ends must not fall apart.[94] We respect minors and infants, disabled children, or people who have grown old at the level of this continuum on which they stand, or we will never respect them. If, on the other hand, the personal dignity of

---

92 Hegel, Georg Wilhelm Friedrich, *Grundlinien der Philosophie des Rechts*, Frankfurt a. M.: Suhrkamp, 1976, 111f.

93 Cf. Spaemann, Robert, *Personen. Versuche über den Unterschied zwischen "etwas" und "jemand"*, Stuttgart: Klett-Cotta, 1996, 196: The word "my kind" as well as the term "person" "does not refer to the similarity of the other person to me, but to the same incomparability and uniqueness. As humans, people are more or less similar. As persons, they are not similar, but the same, for instance in that each one is unique and incommensurable in their dignity."

94 Cf. Dennett, Daniel, "Conditions of Personhood," in: Amélie Oksenberg Rorty (ed.), *The Identities of Persons*, 1976, Berkley / Los Angeles / London: University of California Press, 175–196.

a person depends on the empirical verifiability of his memory and rational faculties, then "being a person" becomes a social label that we attribute to those who meet our expectations of performance. The word "person" then does not express a claim that is removed from our evaluation, but only a social judgement by which we attest to the moral equality of others with ourselves.

Anyone who no longer distinguishes between the empirical concept of personality, into which we all develop only more or less and perhaps not at all, and the idea that every person, regardless of his or her mental and physical performance, is a person who is unavailable to the interests of the other, in the long term, can no longer be certain of his or her own personal dignity. If we link the recognition of personal dignity to the objective proof that the conditions of being a person laid down by social agreement are fulfilled, then everyone must reckon with the fact that they cannot dispel possible doubts even in their own case. We do not do justice to the idea of mutual recognition, which underpins our democratic culture, simply by being generous in granting the relevant personal characteristics for pragmatic reasons and by leaving people with intellectual disabilities or dementia to retain their personal status even though they do not or no longer fulfil the criteria for its attribution. Rather, the connection between intersubjectivity and corporeality is only maintained where we also include the concrete physical existence of the unborn and sick, the old and disabled people in the respect we show for the personhood of all people.

The view held here is often called the equivalence thesis in moral philosophy, as it assumes that the terms "human being" and "person" have an identical scope of application.[95] It does not follow, however, that both terms have the same meaning in every respect. Rather, they must be related to each other in the following way: In terms of their scope of application, the terms "human being" and "person" are identical; they have the same extension, so that no human being can be denied being a person. The equivalence thesis, therefore, rejects any discriminatory unequal treatment that leads to the division of people into different anthropological classes, ranging from the truly human people in the centre to the less human people on the periphery. Nevertheless, the term "person" contains a significant excess of meaning over that of human beings. It focuses on the human being not only as a natural species, but in what distinguishes every human being: in his or her unmistakable identity and singularity. In this respect, the term "person", which incorporates many aspects of the meaning of the classical term "soul", contains a closer definition of the extensionally identical term "human being". Both are congruent in

95 Cf. Birnbacher, Dieter, "Das Dilemma des Personenbegriffs," in: id., *Bioethik zwischen Natur und Interesse*, Frankfurt a. M.: Suhrkamp, 2006, 59.

scope, but the concept of person provides a more precise definition of its meaning than that of the human being.

The accusation of speciesism, which is made against the equivalence thesis, is based on a momentous error: it fails to recognise the importance of the physicality and naturalness of the human being for his concrete personhood. Admittedly, respect for his dignity and the act of mutual recognition are valid for the capacity for moral self-determination, which is also of central importance in the classical understanding of the person. However, it does not follow from this that corporeality and belonging to nature are nothing but mere facticities, which are of no moral significance. Rather, the body is the interface between nature and person, as has been shown in the preceding anthropological considerations. In the body we are integrated into the natural world as members of our biological species; at the same time, the body is the inescapable medium of expression in which we present ourselves as persons in all our acts, in physical activities as well as in the self-execution of the mind. This is the necessary consequence of the fact that the human soul is bodily in nature and cannot express itself otherwise than in bodily gestures. This can also be plausibly explained in the horizon of modern philosophy.

The human being must be regarded as a body-soul unit precisely from the point of view of his moral capacity for action, because his capacity for moral self-determination is given to him no differently than *in* his body and *through* his body. This capacity, which is constitutive for our personhood, does not mean a moral quality that is added to humanity, but rather a specific distinction of humanity, by which it becomes clear what it means to be a human being. Man's mission of moral self-determination cannot be detached from the natural belonging to his own species. For self-determination always takes place under the concrete condition of a natural body, which is, at the same time, the body of the person, the embodiment of a personal self. Since corporeality is one of the necessary conditions of man's subjectivity and moral capacity to act, respect for his personhood must not be shown only to the full expression of self-confidence, rationality, and current self-determination. For "the existence of the body indicates that the necessary conditions for being a person are present."[96] Respect for human dignity must, therefore, encompass the entire field of bodily expression and the temporal continuum that supports and enables the person's spiritual self-realisation. There is no bodily life of a person that is not the life of a person.

This leads to a significant consequence: if nature and person, body and self, biological individual and moral subject are only ever concretely given as an

96 Eurich, Johannes, *Gerechtigkeit für Menschen mit Behinderung. Ethische Reflexionen und sozialpolitische Perspektiven*, Frankfurt a. M. / New York: Campus Verlag, 2008, 291.

inseparable unit, then the very fact that an individual belongs to the human species requires that his or her inviolable dignity and the moral rights deriving from it be recognised unreservedly and in every single case. In the philosophical tradition, the doubling of the terms "human being" and "person" allows for conceptual distinctions, which often lead to misconceptions in the current debate on ethics. Conceptual differentiations must not be understood as dualistic separations that tear apart what belongs together in the lives of physical persons. Rather, *Verena Wetzstein* states: "Only the ability of bodily expression enables the person to fulfil himself. Therefore, the person deserves respect and dignity throughout his or her life."[97] In the past this conviction would have been explained by the fact that every human being, regardless of race, class, gender, or religion, possesses an immortal soul.

Bibliography

Althaus, Paul, *Die letzten Dinge*, Gütersloh: Mohn, [10]1970.

Ammicht-Quinn, Regina, *Körper – Religion – Sexualität. Theologische Reflexionen zur Ethik der Geschlechter*, Mainz: Matthias-Grünewald-Verlag, 1999.

Bachl, Gottfried, "Gedankengänge zur Leiblichkeit," in: Thomas Hoppe (ed.), *Körperlichkeit – Identität. Begegnung in Leiblichkeit*, Freiburg i. Ue.: Academic Press Fribourg, 2008, 143–161.

Birnbacher, Dieter, "Das Dilemma des Personenbegriffs," in: id., *Bioethik zwischen Natur und Interesse*, Frankfurt a. M.: Suhrkamp, 2006, 53–76.

Brunn, Frank Martin, "Biblische Einsichten zur Leib-Seele-Thematik," in: Wilfried Härle (ed.), *Ethik im Kontinuum. Beiträge zur relationalen Erkenntnistheorie und Ontologie*, Marburger theologische Studien 97, Leipzig: Evangelische Verlagsanstalt, 2008, 69–95.

Bultmann, Rudolf, "Der Lebensbegriff des NT," in: Gerhard Kittel (ed.), *Theologisches Wörterbuch zum Neuen Testament*, vol. 2, Stuttgart: W. Kohlhammer, 1935, 862–874.

Bultmann, Rudolf, *Theologie des Neues Testaments*, Tübingen: Mohr, 1977.

Conzelmann, Hans, *Grundriß der Theologie des Neuen Testaments*, Munich: Kaiser, 1967.

Dennett, Daniel, "Conditions of Personhood," in: Amélie Oksenberg Rorty (ed.), *The Identities of Persons*, Berkley / Los Angeles / London: University of California Press, 1976, 175–196.

Dschulnigg, Peter, *Das Markusevangelium*, Theologischer Kommentar zum Neuen Testament 2, Stuttgart: Kohlhammer, 2007.

Dunn, James D.G., *The Theology of Paul the Apostle*, Grand Rapids / Cambridge: Eerdmans, 1998.

Dünzl, Franz, *Geschichte des christologischen Dogmas in der Alten Kirche*, Freiburg i. Br.: Herder, 2019.

Eurich, Johannes, *Gerechtigkeit für Menschen mit Behinderung. Ethische Reflexionen und sozialpolitische Perspektiven*, Frankfurt a. M. / New York: Campus, 2008.

97 Wetzstein, Verena, *Diagnose Alzheimer. Grundlagen einer Ethik der Demenz*, Frankfurt a. M. / New York: Campus Verlag, 2005, 189.

Fichte, Johann Gottlieb, "Die Thatsachen des Bewusstseyns," in: *Fichtes Werke*, vol. 2, ed. I. H. Fichte, Berlin: Veit, 1845/46 (Reprint Berlin, 1971), 535–691.

Gilg, Arnold, *Weg und Bedeutung der altkirchlichen Christologie*, Munich: Kaiser, 1966.

Gilson, Etienne, *History of Christian Philosophy in the Middle Ages*, London: Sheed and Ward, 1955.

Gilson, Etienne, *Le Thomisme. Introduction à la Philosophie de Saint Thomas*, Paris: Vrin, 71979.

Gögler, Rolf, *Zur Theologie des biblischen Wortes bei Origenes*, Düsseldorf: Patmos, 1963.

Greshake, Gisbert, "Das Verhältnis 'Unsterblichkeit der Seele' und 'Auferstehung des Leibes' in problemgeschichtlicher Sicht," in: id. / Gerhard Lohfink (eds.), *Naherwartung – Auferstehung – Unsterblichkeit*, Quaestiones disputatae 71, Freiburg i. Br.: Herder, 1975, 82–120.

Greshake, Gisbert / Kremer, Jakob, *Resurrectio mortuorum. Zum theologischen Verständnis der leiblichen Auferstehung*, Darmstadt: Wissenschaftliche Buchgesellschaft, 1986.

Greshake, Gisbert, "Zwischenzustand," in: *Lexikon für Theologie und Kirche*, vol. 10, Freiburg i. Br.: Herder, 32001, 1529–1531.

Grillmeier, Alois, *Jesus der Christus im Glauben der Kirche*, vol. 1: *Von der apostolischen Zeit bis zum Konzil von Chalzedon* (451), Freiburg i. Br.: Herder, 1979.

Groß, Walter, "Die Gottebenbildlichkeit des Menschen im Kontext der Priesterschrift," *Theologische Quartalschrift* 161 (1981), 244–265.

Hastedt, Heiner, *Das Leib-Seele-Problem*, Berlin: Suhrkamp, 1988.

Harder, Günther / Schnelle, Udo, "Seele. I–II," in: Lothar Coenen / Klaus Haacker (eds.), *Theologisches Begriffslexikon zum Neuen Testament*, vol. 2, Wuppertal: R. Brockhaus, 2000, 1617–1621.

Hegel, Georg Wilhelm Friedrich, *Grundlinien der Philosophie des Rechts*, Frankfurt a. M.: Suhrkamp, 1976.

Hoping, Helmut, *Jesus aus Galiläa. Messias und Sohn Gottes*, Freiburg i. Br.: Herder, 2019.

Husserl, Edmund, *Cartesianische Meditationen. Die Krisis der europäischen Wissenschaften und die transzendentale Phänomenologie*, Gesammelte Schriften 8, Hamburg: Meiner, 1992.

Hünermann, Peter (ed.), *Die Dokumente des Zweiten Vatikanischen Konzils*, vol. 1, Freiburg: Herder, 2004.

van Imschoot, Paul, "Seele," in: Herbert Haag (ed.), *Bibellexikon*, Einsiedeln: Benziger 1968, 1564–1568.

Irsigler, Hubert, "Die Frage nach dem Menschen in Ps 8. Zu Bedeutung und Horizont eines kontroversen Menschenbildes im Alten Testament," in: id., *Vom Adamssohn zum Immanuel*, St. Ottilien: EOS, 1997, 1–48.

Janowski, Bernd, *Konfliktgespräche mit Gott. Eine Anthropologie der Psalmen*, Neukirchen-Vluyn: Neukirchener Verlag, 2003.

Janowski, Bernd, "Der Mensch im alten Israel. Grundfragen alttestamentlicher Anthropologie," *Zeitschrift für Theologie und Kirche* 102 (2005), 173–175.

Kaiser, Otto, *Der Gott des Alten Testaments: Wesen und Wirken*, Theologie des AT 2, Göttingen: Vandenhoeck & Ruprecht, 1998.

Kany, Roland, "Christologie im antiken Christentum," in: Karlheinz Ruhstorfer (ed.), *Christologie*, Paderborn: Schöningh, 2018, 141–213.

Kaulbach, Friedrich, "Leib/Körper. II. Neuzeit," in: Joachim Ritter / Karlfried Gründer (eds.), *Historisches Wörterbuch der Philosophie*, vol. 5, Basel / Stuttgart: Schwabe & Co., 1980, 178–185.

Kather, Regine, *Person. Die Begründung menschlicher Identität*, Darmstadt: Wissenschaftliche Buchgesellschaft, 2007.

Kostka, Ulrike, *Der Mensch in Krankheit, Heilung und Gesundheit im Spiegel der modernen Medizin. Eine biblische und theologisch-ethische Reflexion*, Münster: LIT, 1999.

Kuhse, Helga, *The Sanctity-of-Life-Doctrine in Medicine*, Oxford: Clarendon Press, 1987.

Kutschmann, Werner, *Der Naturwissenschaftler und sein Körper*, Frankfurt a. M.: Suhrkamp, 1982.
Langemeyer, Georg, "Seele," in: Wolfgang Beinert (ed.), *Lexikon der katholischen Dogmatik*, Freiburg i. Br.: Herder, 1991, 465.
Van Meegen, Sven, *Alttestamentliche Ethik als Grundlage einer heutigen Lebensethik. Ein Beitrag zum interreligiösen Dialog*, Münster: LIT, 2005.
Marcel, Gabriel, "Sein, Haben, Hoffnung," in: id., *Hoffnung in einer zerbrochenen Welt? Vorlesungen und Aufsätze*, Werkauswahl 1, Paderborn: Schöningh, 1992, 59–103.
Marcel, Gabriel, *Metaphysisches Tagebuch 1915–1943*, Werkauswahl 2, Paderborn: Schöningh, 1992.
Moltmann, Jürgen, *Theologie der Hoffnung. Untersuchungen zur Begründung und zu den Konsequenzen einer christlichen Eschatologie*, Munich: Kaiser, ^{9}1973.
Pfeiffer, Matthias, *Einweisung in das neue Sein. Neutestamentliche Erwägungen zur Grundlegung der Ethik*, Beiträge zur evangelischen Theologie 119, Gütersloh: Gütersloher Verlagshaus, 2002.
Pieper, Josef, "Unsterblichkeit – eine nicht-christliche Vorstellung? Philosophische Bemerkungen zu einem kontroverstheologischen Thema (1959)," in: id., *Religionsphilosophische Schriften*, Werke in acht Bänden 7, ed. Berthold Wald, Hamburg: Meiner, 2000, 291–313.
Pieper, Josef, *Tod und Unsterblichkeit*, Munich: Kösel, 1968.
Plessner, Helmuth, "Lachen und Weinen. Eine Untersuchung der Grenzen menschlichen Verhaltens," in: id., *Ausdruck und menschliche Natur*, Gesammelte Schriften 7, Frankfurt a. M.: Suhrkamp, 1982, 201–388.
Ratzinger, Joseph, *Eschatologie – Tod und ewiges Leben*, Regensburg: Pustet, ^{2}1977.
Reinmuth, Eckart, *Anthropologie im Neuen Testament*, Tübingen: Francke, 2006.
Runggaldier, Edmund, "Unsterblichkeitshoffnung und die hylemorphistische Einheit von Leib und Seele," in: Karl-Ludwig Koenen / Josef Schuster (eds.), *Seele oder Hirn? Vom Leben und Überleben der Personen nach dem Tod*, Münster: Aschendorff, 2012, 95–123.
Scharbert, Josef, *Fleisch, Geist und Seele im Pentateuch*, Stuttgarter Bibelstudien 19, Stuttgart: Verlag Katholisches Bibelwerk, 1966.
Schelkle, Karl Hermann, *Theologie des Neuen Testaments*, vol. 3: *Ethos*, Düsseldorf: Patmos, 1970.
Schipperges, Heinrich / Pfeil, Hans, *Der menschliche Leib aus medizinischer und philosophischer Sicht*, Aschaffenburg: Pattloch, 1984.
Schmidt, Werner H., "Anthropologische Begriffe im Alten Testament," *Evangelische Theologie* 24 (1964), 375–388.
Schmithals, Walter, *Die theologische Anthropologie des Paulus*, Stuttgart: Kohlhammer, 1980.
Schnelle, Udo, "Seele. III," in: Lothar Coenen / Klaus Haacker (eds.), *Theologisches Begriffslexikon zum Neuen Testament*, vol. 2, Wuppertal: R. Brockhaus, 2000, 1621–1626.
Schockenhoff, Eberhard, *Zum Fest der Freiheit. Theologie des christlichen Handelns bei Origenes*, Mainz: Matthias-Grünewald-Verlag, 1990.
Schöpf, Alfred, "Das Leib-Seele-Problem in phänomenologischer Sicht," in: Karl-E. Bühler (ed.), *Aspekte des Leib-Seele-Problems. Philosophie, Medizin, Künstliche Intelligenz*, Würzburg: Königshausen und Naumann, 1980, 193–205.
Schroer, Silvia / Staubli, Thomas, *Die Körpersymbolik der Bibel*, Gütersloh: Gütersloher Verlagshaus, 2005.
Seebaß, Horst, "Leben II. Altes Testament," in: Theologische Realenzyklopädie, vol. 20, Berlin: Walter de Gruyter, 1990, 520–524.
Spaemann, Robert, *Personen. Versuche über den Unterschied zwischen "etwas" und "jemand"*, Stuttgart: Klett-Cotta, 1996.
Stenger, Wolfgang, "Die Gottesbezeichnung 'lebendiger Gott' im Neuen Testament," *Trierer theologische Zeitschrift 87* (1978), 61–69.

Strack, Hermann L. / Billerbeck, Paul, *Das Evangelium nach Matthäus erläutert aus Talmud und Midrasch*, Kommentar zum Neuen Testament aus Talmud und Midrasch 1, Munich: C.H.Beck, 1922.
Vollenweider, Samuel, "Der Menschgewordene als Ebenbild Gottes. Zum frühchristlichen Verständnis der Imago Dei," in: Hans-Peter Mathys (ed.), *Ebenbild Gottes – Herrscher über die Welt. Studien zu Würde und Auftrag des Menschen*, Neukirchen-Vluyn: Neukirchener Verlag, 1998, 123–146.
Waldenfels, Bernhard, *Das leibliche Selbst*, Frankfurt a. M.: Suhrkamp, ^{3}2006.
Westermann, Claus, *Genesis*, vol. 1: Genesis 1–11, Biblischer Kommentar Altes Testament I/1, Neukirchen-Vluyn: Neukirchener Verlag, ^{2}1976.
Wetzstein, Verena, *Diagnose Alzheimer. Grundlagen einer Ethik der Demenz*, Frankfurt a. M. / New York: Campus, 2005.
Williams, Bernard, "Personenidentität und Individuation," in: id., *Probleme des Selbst. Philosophische Aufsätze 1956–1972*, trans. J. Schulte, Stuttgart: Reclam, 1978, 7–36.
Wolff, Hans Werner, *Anthropologie des Alten Testaments*, Gütersloh: Gütersloher Verlagshaus, 2002.
Wucherer-Huldenfeld, Augustinus K., "Das Miteinander als Zugang zum Leib-Seele-Problem," in: Günther Pöltner / Helmuth Vetter (eds.), *Leben zur Gänze. Das Leib-Seele-Problem*, Vienna / Munich: Herold, 1986, 27–48.

Suggestions for Further Reading[98]

Goetz, Stewart / Taliaferro, Charles, *A Brief History of the Soul*, Chichester: Wiley-Blackwell, 2011.
Janowski, Bernd / Schwöbel, Christoph (eds.), *Gott – Seele – Welt. Interdisziplinäre Beiträge zur Rede von der Seele*, Theologie Interdisziplinär 14, Neukirchen-Vluyn: Neukirchener Verlagsgesellschaft, 2013.
Murphy, Nancey, *Bodies and Souls, or Spirited Bodies?*, Current Issues in Theology 3, Cambridge: Cambridge University Press, 2006.
Wright, John P. / Potter, Paul (eds.), *Psyche and Soma. Physicians and metaphysicians on the mind-body problem from Antiquity to Enlightenment*, Oxford: Clarendon Press, 2000.

98 By the editors.

Bernhard Uhde

The Concept of Soul in Islam

„O thou soul at peace!
Enter My Garden.“[1]

A Preliminary Methodological Remark

Discussions about "Islam" seem to fail to recognise that Islam is very diverse in terms of its history and expansion, and that it is developing quite differently in the present. This diversity is not only due to the plurality of legal schools of the Sunna as well as the different denominations of the Shia and other schools, i.e. in the field of religious scholarship, but also to very different individual religious practices or practices that invoke religious justifications, which cannot be applied to Islam as a whole.[2] However, since it is not possible to draw conclusions about the general from the particular,[3] overall statements about "Islam" are only accurate if their negation led to exclusion from all schools of law and faiths, such as the negation of Muhammad's prophethood or the existence of God.[4] With all other statements, their generalisations are therefore to be avoided, even if their limited scope is not explicitly pointed out.

In regard to discussions about the "concept of the soul in Islam", these references apply in the same way. What does "soul" mean, what does "Islam" mean? Different understandings of what is called "soul" (*nafs*) can be found in the different directions and schools of Islam. Another problem arises. The conceptions of what is often rendered as "soul" in the English language, which are influenced by Greek philosophy on the one hand, and by Jewish and Christian tradition on the other hand, have different names in the Greek, Hebrew[5] and Arabic languages.

1 Qur'an 89:27,30. Translation (and all following Qur'an translations) from: Nasr, Seyyed Hossein (ed.), *The Study Quran. A New Translation and Commentary*, New York: Harper Collins, 2016.

2 Example of such a practice: the Taliban of Afghanistan.

3 As Aristotle has previously said, *Anal. Post.* 91 b 34 f.

4 Example of such a negation: "Muhammad was neither a prophet nor did he have anything at all to do with God, because God does not exist."

5 Cf. also Rösel, Martin, "Die Geburt der Seele in der Übersetzung: von der hebräischen näfäsch über die psyche der LXX zur deutschen Seele," in: Andreas Wagner (ed.), *Anthropologische Aufbrüche: Alttestamentliche und interdisziplinäre Zugänge zur historischen Anthropologie*, Forschungen

https://doi.org/10.1515/9783110748239-003

Thus, the Arabic word *rūḥ*, like *nafs*, is not infrequently translated as "soul",[6] although in the case of both words, the translation can and must be questioned, for

> Islamic theology uses the words *nafs* (fem.) and *rūh* (gen. comm.) where we say "soul" or "spirit". However, we must bear in mind that the concepts behind the words *nafs-rūh* are not the same as those we associate with our terms soul-spirit. This follows, among other things, from the fact that Christian theology regards the soul, the spirit, as something essentially different from the body, as a being that belongs to a higher level among creatures, the so-called spirit beings, to which the angels also belong. In Islam, however, there is no dogma of the spirituality of the soul in the sense of Christian dogmatics; whether the soul of man (*nafs-rūh*) is a spiritual or corporeal being is rather a matter of dispute in Muslim theology, and no Muslim may therefore be denied orthodoxy because he professes the spirituality or corporeality of the *nafs*.[7]

This difficulty in translating the words and contents of world religions is a problem of the human language.[8] All religions, including the world religions, naturally first use the language that was spoken in the environment of the emergence and early expansion of the respective religion. Two problems are to be noted here: on the one hand, the local limitation of each language within the multitude of human languages and, on the other hand, the temporal determination of the respective language as the language of a certain time. This gives rise to the problem of disseminating and/or translating the original language into other linguistic and cultural areas, on the one hand, and the problem of transferring the original language into the respective present, on the other. Both problems are interconnected, especially since translations of religious texts and descriptions of religious phenomena usually have a content that does not originate from the time of the translator or the describer.[9]

But even with an error-free translation, should it be possible, the sound of the language and the melody of the original language are largely lost. As an example for other sacred texts, this is pointed out by Muslims particularly in translations of the Qur'an: regardless of the question of whether the Qur'an, which is written in Arabic and which is, in the self-understanding of Islam, the language of God, can and should be translated into another language at all, the speech melody contained

---

zur Religion und Literatur des Alten und Neuen Testaments 232, Göttingen: Vandenhoeck & Ruprecht, 2009, 151–170.

6 Cf. e.g. the German title of the "Kitāb ar-Rūḥ" by Ibn Qayyim al-Ǧawziyya, *Die menschliche Seele*, trans. Alper Soytürk, Fulda: independently published, 2020; and many more.

7 Stieglecker, Hermann, *Die Glaubenslehren des Islam. Neuedition der Auflage von 1983*, Paderborn: Schöningh, 2021, 687.

8 Cf. Wendt, Reinhard (ed.), W*ege durch Babylon. Missionare, Sprachstudien und interkulturelle Kommunikation*, Tübingen: Narr, 1998; Krienke, Markus, *Theologie – Philosophie – Sprache. Einführung in das theologische Denken Antonio Rosminis*, Regensburg: Friedrich Pustet, 2006.

9 Cf. Uhde, Bernhard, *Warum sie glauben, was sie glauben. Weltreligionen für Andersgläubige und Nachdenkende*, Freiburg: Herder, 2013, 29 ff.

in the Qur'an recitation can hardly be reproduced in another language. The attempt to translate is similar to the attempt to perform a German prose translation of a text originally composed for the score of an Italian opera. In the case of the Qur'anic recitation, however, this also means no small loss of religious feeling and spirituality,[10] and to these are added the differences in sound perception.[11]

But even the words themselves have different meanings, even if a translation tried to convey them accurately. Both Arabic-speaking Muslims and Arabic-speaking Christians use the Arabic word for "God" in colloquial language, in prayer, and worship: *Allāh*. And yet: despite the word equivalence, the Christian should believe and think of "God" as a Trinity, whereas the Muslim should not, but as an absolute unity. Here, the important difference of "univocation" and "equivocation" should be noted. Thus, the word "God" is the same for the Jew, the Christian, and the Muslim, but it is to be understood equivocally. Also the designation, "Abrahamic religions", for Judaism, Christianity, and Islam sometimes conceals the fact that "Abraham" is not to be understood here as univocation, but as equivocation.[12]

These few references are intended to signify that the concept of the soul in Islam can only be presented here as an example, a concept as it arises from the tradition of Greek philosophy as well as the criticism of Islam with regard to Judaism and Christianity. Therefore, this criticism is to be addressed in order to trace the reception of Greek philosophy and the corrective adoption of Jewish and Christian conceptions of the soul in the Qur'an and Hadith, in theology, philosophy and mysticism.

1 Islam as the Restoration of the Uncorrupted and Non-Self-Contradictory Religion

Islam is the realisation of the experience of the speech of the One God who created everything, sustains everything, and completes everything. This One God enters into a special relationship with all people by letting them hear from Him through prophets. The revelation given to all people through the Prophet Muhammad (ca. 570–632) is the extended restoration of previous revelations, especially of the Torah and the

---

10 Cf. Uhde, Bernhard, "Zur Einführung," in: *Der Koran*, ed. Bernhard Uhde, trans. Ahmad Milad Karimi, Freiburg: Herder, 2009, 526 ff.

11 Cf. Volke, Stefan, *Sprachphysiognomik. Grundlagen einer leibphänomenologischen Beschreibung der Lautwahrnehmung*, Freiburg: Karl Alber, 2007.

12 Cf. also Halft, Dennis, "Abrahami(ti)sche Religionen," *Wort und Antwort. Dominikanische Zeitschrift für Glauben und Gesellschaft* 62, 4 (2021), 146 f.

Gospel, which were falsified by the followers of the respective prophetic bearers of revelation, Moses and Jesus, through additions (*taḥrīf*).

This is the fundamental systematic self-determination of Islam, which sees itself as an analytically expanded restoration of the pure religion as it already existed as the "creed of Abraham"[13] and was confirmed by further concordant revelations:

> We [i.e. the Muslims] believe in God, and in that which was sent down unto us, and in that which was sent down unto Abraham, Ishmael, Isaac, Jacob, and the Tribes, and in what Moses and Jesus were given, and in what the prophets were given from their Lord. We make no distinction among any of them, and unto Him [i.e. God] we submit.[14]

Thus, the revelation that Moses and Jesus received is also true – but falsified by the followers of the respective prophets, i.e. by Jews, on the one hand, and Christians, on the other. If in Judaism the assertion of the particular election of the people of Israel is a falsifying violation of God's true, universal, and equal grant of salvation to all people and, thus, a disregard of God's universality and justice, then in Christianity the emergence of Christology is to be regarded as a violation of God's absoluteness and mercy, because Christology is regarded as self-contradictory and, thus, as incomprehensible, and, therefore, represents a disregard of God's mercy. The pure religion of Abraham is therefore to be returned to:

> O People of the Book [i.e. Jews and Christians]! Why do you dispute concerning Abraham, as neither the Torah nor the Gospel was sent down until after him? Do you not understand? Behold! You are the very same who dispute concerning that of which you have knowledge; so why do you dispute concerning that of which you have no knowledge? God knows, and you know not. Abraham was neither Jew nor Christian, but rather was a *ḥanīf*, a submitter, and he was not one of the idolaters.[15]

Both falsifications as violations of God's universality and absoluteness are eradicated by Islam and, thus, the true respect for God's justice and mercy is restored through the collection of the revelation passed through Muhammad, the literal Word of God, the Qur'an, "that which is to be repeated". The core contents of the Qur'an are the doctrine of the absolute sublimity of God[16] and the absolute unity of God,[17] both of which are presented against Christology, in particular, and the

13 Qur'an 2:135.
14 Qur'an 2:136; 3:84. Cf. 4:163 f., 6:83 ff., 37:75 ff. a.o.
15 Qur'an 3:65–67.
16 Cf. Qur'an 42:11 a.o.
17 Cf. Qur'an 4:36 a.o.

doctrine of the Trinity of Christian theology,[18] and the Love of God for all people,[19] this, in particular, against the idea of the election of Judaism. Man is to respond to this love of God through "Islam", "submission", "devotion", i.e. complete surrender of one's own will to the Will of God, by remembering God's words as continuously as possible and following them as far as he can understand them. The expression of this response is the observance of a multitude of high ethical commandments and prohibitions, which culminate in love for God and love for people.

This brief characterisation of Islam does not immediately make clear the methodological principle with which Islam, and, thus, the Qur'an itself and Islamic theology, make themselves known to people. Islam sees itself as a religion of understanding,[20] of rational knowledge that is accessible and evident to every human being because it is a natural principle of understanding. Every human being is, therefore, naturally apt to an insight that is formulated in Greek philosophy as the first and most certain principle of thought for all human beings in the "law of non-contradiction": "It is impossible for the same attribute at once to belong and not to belong to the same thing and in the same relation".[21] It is, therefore, impossible to attribute self-contradictory predicates to the same subject or issue at the same time and in completely the same respect, because then no statement is made. The certainty of this principle of understanding results from the impossibility of its refutation: anyone who wants to attribute the predicate "false!" to this principle does not want to say "true!" at the same time and in the same respect – he, thus, presupposes the content of the proposition to be true when attempting to refute it.[22]

This supreme and most certain principle of knowledge of understanding, which can be raised to Aristotle[23] as a formal principle of Greek philosophy with a known prehistory, is applied in principle in Islam, because Islam as a religion[24]

---

18 Cf. Qur'an 5:72 f. a.o.

19 Cf. Qur'an 5:54 a.o.

20 Cf. also Karimi, Ahmad Milad, *Licht über Licht. Dekonstruktion des religiösen Denkens im Islam*, falsafa. Horizonte islamischer Religionsphilosophie 1, Freiburg / Munich: Karl Alber, 2021, 143 ff.: "Der Islam als eine Religion des Verstandes".

21 Aristotle, *Metaphysics* 1005 b 19 f. Trans. H. Tredennick, Cambridge, MA / London: Harvard University Press, 1989, 161.

22 Cf. Aristotle's interpretation, Aristotle, *Metaphysics* 1005 b 19 f, 161.

23 Cf. Uhde, Bernhard, *Erste Philosophie und menschliche Unfreiheit. Studien zur Geschichte der Ersten Philosophie*, Part I, Wiesbaden: Franz Steiner, 1976, 70 f.

24 "Islam" as the surrender of the human will to God is the principle of all principles of human action in all areas, and, thus, also in religion, but not only in religion: "altogether, however, a habitus that leaves out no area" (Uhde, Bernhard, "'Kein Zwang in der Religion' (Koran 2,256). Zum Problem von Gewaltpotential und Gewalt in den 'monotheistischen' Weltreligionen," *Jahrbuch für Religionsphilosophie* 2 (2003), 85 f.)

is based on God's merciful responsiveness to all human beings and is, thus, understood as a responsiveness to the natural human mind: "God has indeed commissioned the prophets to speak to people according to their understanding."[25] And every human mind – unlike those animals that are deaf and dumb[26] – is naturally oriented towards Islam,[27] and those who consider Islam to be "mockery and play" are "people who do not understand."[28]

This conclusion is also significant for the concept of the soul in Islam because this concept seeks to present a self-contradiction-free knowledge of understanding, as demanded by the "law of non-contradiction". Such knowledge is conveyed by Greek philosophy, especially Aristotle's writing, "On the Soul" (*Peri psychês*),[29] which itself is the result of a tradition. Together with traditions from Judaism and Christianity, basic features of a concept of the soul emerge in Islam, in that the knowledge of understanding, which is understood as free of self-contradiction, is connected with the idea of the creation of the soul by God, as he is believed in Judaism and Christianity to be the creator of souls.

2 Traditions: Philosophy and Religion: *Psyché, Nefesh, Ruaḥ, Anima*

The tradition of early Greek thought corresponds to a history of the development of knowledge.[30] The concept of the "soul" (*psyché*)[31] also experiences such a history of development. In the oldest Greek poetry, in Homer, this term is already encountered in the proem of the "Odyssey", when a song about Odysseus, who

25 Muhammad al-Ġazzālī, cited in Gramlich, Richard, *Muḥammad al-Ġazzālīs Lehre von den Stufen zur Gottesliebe. Die Bücher 31–36 seines Hauptwerkes eingeleitet, übersetzt und kommentiert*, Wiesbaden: Franz Steiner, 1984, 537.

26 Cf. Qur'an 8:22.

27 Cf. Qur'an 30:30: "Set thy face as a *ḥanīf*, in the primordial nature from God upon which He originated mankind".

28 Qur'an 5:58 a.o.

29 On this, see Gätje, Helmut, *Studien zur Überlieferung der aristotelischen Psychologie im Islam*, Heidelberg: Winter, 1971; also: Gara, Nizar Samir, *Die Rezeption der Philosophie des Aristoteles im Islam: als Beispiel die Rezeption der Seelenlehre des Aristoteles bei Ibn Sīnās Buch (Ilm al-nafs: Die Wissenschaft der Seele)*, PhD Thesis, Heidelberg, 2003.

30 The following explanations are limited to a few aspects for a better understanding of the peculiarity of the conception of the "soul" in Islam.

31 Cf. Meyer, Martin F., "Der Wandel des Psyche-Begriffs im frühgriechischen Denken von Homer bis Heraklit," *Archiv für Begriffsgeschichte* 50 (2008), 9 ff.

tries to save his *psyché* despite all the dangers, is sung.[32] Here, *psyché* can be translated as and equated with "life", in that the *psyché* is the principle of the self-movement of a body living in this body; therefore, it is the *psyché* that one presents to death in battle.[33] Death, however, is immobility, complete loss of self-movement, for at death the soul leaves this body to lead a shadowy existence in an underworld.[34] This, however, provides a continuity of the soul beyond death, as also taught by the Orphics and Pythagoras, albeit in connection with a doctrine of rebirth. Plato takes up the idea of the continuity of the psyche when he conceives the *psyché* as self-moving, but, therefore, also as immortal.[35] And it has not "become", since it is self-moving,[36] because movement of the living, the soul, cannot be produced by something motionless, this would be a self-contradiction. Therefore, the soul, itself incorporeal, can also live without a body, that is, independently of this body, which it leaves again at its death.[37]

Aristotle, on the other hand, in his writing, "On the Soul" (*Peri psychês*), defines the psyche exclusively in relation to the human body: "So the soul must be substance [*ousía*] in the sense of being the form of a natural body, which potentially has life. And substance in this sense is actuality [*entelécheia*]. The soul, then, is the actuality of the kind of body we have described."[38] Therefore, the soul is obviously connected to the human body: "It is quite clear, then, that neither the soul nor certain parts of it [. . .] can be separated from the body".[39] Since this connection of the soul is the completion, the realisation of the body's possibility of life, it is, itself incorporeally, indissolubly connected with this body and cannot live without it. Thus, as a pure form, it is the principle of the movement of this body, both of its pure movement and of its spiritual and sensual possibilities. Together with the body, the soul determines the individual living being in all its possibilities and their realisations, thus, also in its singularity, in itself.

32 Homer, *Odyssey* I, 5.

33 Cf. Homer, *Iliad* 9, 322.

34 Cf. Homer, *Odyssey* XI, 37.

35 Cf. Plato, *Phaidros* 245 c; cf. *Nomoi* 896 a f. On this, see Enders, Markus, "Das Leben als Prinzip der Selbstbewegung – zum Verständnis des Lebens in der Philosophie der Antike, in der christlichen Bibel und der Philosophie des lateinischen Mittelalters," in: Franziska Neufeld / Chiara Pasqualin / Anne Kirstine Rønhede / Sihan Wu (eds.), *Leben in lebendigen Fragen. Zwischen Kontinuität und Pluralität*, Freiburg / Munich: Karl Alber, 2021, 30 f.

36 Plato, *Phaidros* 246 a.

37 Cf. Plato, *Phaidon* 79 c 1 ff. Plato's doctrine of the parts of the soul will not be discussed here.

38 Aristotle, *On the soul* 412 a 19–22. Trans. W.S. Hett, London: Harvard University Press, 1975, 69.

39 Aristotle, *On the soul* 413 a 4 f.; 73.

The two views of Plato and Aristotle show similarities with regard to the soul as self-movement and other properties but differ in their respective relationship to the body. In later times, the soul is often understood as a corporeal or incorporeal carrier of movement, including the movements of incorporeal feeling, willing, and thinking, as life. The difficulties of differentiating the soul from the material body (*sôma*), on the one hand, and from the mental faculty of thought (*noũs*), on the other hand, were solved in different ways in different schools, so that no uniform finding can be discerned. Thus, Greek tradition offers one word, *psyché*, but a number of interpretations and translations of this word.

Jewish tradition, beginning with the Torah, knows two terms that are often translated as "soul": *nefesh* and *ruaḥ*. Both have a long history of development, both hit the word "soul" only inaccurately, although this word itself must be understood as an equivocation. At the beginning of the Torah, the word *nefesh* ("soul") is also connected with the epithet *ḥaja* ("living"),[40] so that the meaning "living being" suggests itself. This meaning shows a relationship to the early Greek conception, because both *nefesh* and *psyché* denote the life of the living body, and are, therefore, connected with this body, so that *nefesh* can also be translated as "life".[41] Since the root of the word *nefesh* can be associated with "breath", "breathing", but since breathing is a characteristic of life and, thus, self-movement, the movement of breathing and its pacification is also an expression for resting on the Sabbath.[42] *Nefesh* denotes the whole, self-moving, living person, the connection of soul and body; a *nefesh* is never without or outside a body. At the same time, however, it also has the ability of movement of an incorporeal kind, especially of the will, directed towards "worldly things" such as hunger and thirst,[43] or sexuality,[44] but also towards God.[45] But *nefesh* is always the form or content of living movement, which also leads to the possibility of designating the body or parts of the body. In later, Hellenistic times, this "soul", following Plato's school, is understood as immortal, as it is created by God himself.[46] Therefore, in the "world to come", this soul, detached from the body, is subjected to the judgement of God's justice for its behaviour in the here and now, as taught in the

40 Cf. Gen 1:20; 2:7. a.o.
41 Cf. Gen 19:20.
42 Cf. Exod 23:12; cf. 31:17.
43 Cf. Deut 12:15 a.o.
44 Cf. Gen 34:3 a.o.
45 Especially in the Psalms, cf. Ps 63:2; 84:3 a.o.
46 On this, see Heckel, Theo K., "Die Seele im hellenistischen Judentum und frühem Christentum," in: Georg Gasser / Josef Quitterer (eds.), *Die Aktualität des Seelenbegriffs. Interdisziplinäre Zugänge*, Paderborn: Schöningh, 2010, 327 f.

eschatology of the Ethiopian Book of Enoch,[47] a justice that is not opposed to God's mercy. This interrelation of God's justice and mercy is an interrelation reserved for God, so that the two modes of action are not thought of separately but always together, as a Jewish parable teaches:

> The Lord God made the earth and the heavens [Genesis 2:4]. A parable of a king who had two goblets of fine glass. The king said, "If I pour hot water into them, they will (expand and) burst; if cold water, they will contract (and break)." What did he do? He mixed hot and cold water and poured it into them, and so they remained unbroken. Similarly, the saint said: "If I create the world with the quality of mercy alone, its sins would be too many; if with righteousness alone, how can it be expected to endure? So I will create it with both justice and mercy, and it may endure!"[48]

It is not easy to distinguish *ruaḥ* from *nefesh*. Thus, in a parallelism it says: ". . . and what is my soul among all the spirits . . ."[49] If *nefesh* can be translated as "soul", *ruaḥ* can be translated as "spirit", "breath". This "spirit" is a special "life force" for man, which is added to the *nefesh* by God.[50] God breathes this life-force into the nostrils of humans[51] and other living creatures[52] as "breath of life", so that they come to life, to breathe and to have special strength. This very power can also disappear:

> But when the queen of Sheba saw all the wisdom of Solomon, and the house which he had built, and the food for his table, and the seating of his great ones, and the waiting of his servants, and their garments, and his cupbearers, and his burnt offerings which he offered in the house of the Lord, her breath [*ruaḥ*] caught.[53]

The power of *ruaḥ* is, therefore, a power in motion. If *nefesh* is the possibility of self-movement of the body, *ruaḥ* is the God-given possibility of a particular powerful movement – so also in the meaning "wind",[54] which is "created by God"[55] – or its loss. In this respect, *nefesh* and *ruaḥ* are not synonymous, but related: both

---

47 Cf. 1 Enoch 22:1–4.

48 *Genesis Rabba* 12:15.

49 Sir 16:17.

50 The relationship between *nefesh* and *ruaḥ* is reminiscent of the ancient Greek idea of the relationship between *psyché* and *thymós*; on this, see Uhde, Bernhard, "PSYCHE – EIN SYMBOL? Zum Verständnis von Leben und Tod im frühgriechischen Denken," in: Gunther Stephenson (ed.), *Leben und Tod in den Religionen. Symbol und Wirklichkeit,* Darmstadt: Wissenschaftliche Buchgesellschaft, 1985, 108 f.; on Jewish tradition, see Johnson, Aubrey R., *The Vitality of the Individual in the Thought of Ancient Israel,* Cardiff: University of Wales Press, 1949, 28 ff.

51 Cf. Gen 2:7.

52 Cf. Gen 7:22.

53 1 Kgs 10:4 f.

54 Cf. Isa 40:7.

55 Cf. Amos 4:13.

incorporeal, both in motion, both connected to the body – and yet differentiated, in that *ruaḥ* takes hold of the human being, *nefesh* constitutes the human being. In the interaction of both, powerful life arises, movement of the body, the soul, and the spirit.

The Christian tradition takes up elements of Judaism and Hellenistic Judaism with the influence of Greek philosophy as well as elements of Roman thought for the definition of "soul". This tradition finds expression in the writings of Augustine,[56] in the work, "De anima et eius origine libri quattuor". Early on, Augustine had expressed his special interest in the soul; in the "Soliloquia", when asked by reason: "Quid ergo scire vis?", he replies: "Deum et animam scire cupio [. . .] nihil omnino."[57] So what is this "soul"? Augustine had read "books by Platonists"[58] and was impressed by them, also with regard to the doctrines of the soul. In addition, in contrast to Greek and Jewish thought and in transition to Christian thought, Augustine understands:[59] The soul, like everything created by God, is created by God out of nothing to live a unique life in the body (against Plato[60]). It is also not a hypostasis of God's Spirit or of the One (against Plotinus[61]). The soul is completely incorporeal (against Tertullian[62]) and immortal (against Aristotle[63]) because it is independent of the body (against early Jewish tradition[64]). Thus, this doctrine, in its difference from other conceptions, becomes the doctrine proper to this kind of Christian theology.

The philosophical, Jewish, and Christian teachings of the soul are adopted into the Islamic tradition.

---

56 On this, see also Grabmann, Martin, *Die Grundgedanken des heiligen Augustinus über die Seele und Gott*, Darmstadt: Wissenschaftliche Buchgesellschaft, 1967, and Enders, "Leben als Prinzip der Selbstbewegung," 51f.

57 Augustine, *Soliloquorum libri duo* I, 7. Both writings "De quantitate animae" and "De immortalitate animae" were written 387 CE, as well as the "Soliloquia" (cf. *Soliloquorum libri duo* I, 17).

58 Augustine, *Confessiones* VII, 9, (13); cf. *De civitate Dei* VIII, 12.

59 Cf. Augustine, *De genesi ad litteram* 7 a.o.

60 Cf. Plato, *Phaidros* 245 a 1 f. a.o.

61 Cf. Plotinus, *Enneads* IV.

62 Cf. Tertullian, *De anima* cap. VI. On this, see Kitzler, Petr, "Nihil enim anima si non corpus. Tertullian und die Körperlichkeit der Seele," *Wiener Studien 122* (2009), 145 ff.

63 Cf. Aristotle, *Peri psychês* 413 a 4 f.

64 Cf. Gen 19:20 a.o.

3 A "Concept of Soul" in the Qur'an?

Islam, as a pure doctrine, addresses the human mind, which is supposed to recognise the non-self-contradictory nature of this doctrine, especially the non-self-contradictory nature of the Qur'an. Although the Qur'an does not use the noun *'aql* – "understanding", the verb form *'aqala* – "to understand", "to think" is used forty-nine times, nineteen of which are in connection with faith.[65]

Only Islam, then, presents truth without contradiction, a truth that can be seen by anyone endowed with understanding.[66] Thus, Islam also sees itself as a religion that was revealed to the natural understanding of all people. God speaks about Himself in the Qur'an, and He gives examples in the Prophet Muhammad and the prophets. This does not exceed the natural understanding, and, thus, the ethics of Islam are comprehensible as a practice because they are grounded in understanding. Therefore, the text of the Qur'an should also be free of contradiction; what might appear to the mind as a contradiction is abrogated by the doctrine of abrogation[67] (*nasḫ*) with reference to the Qur'anic verse: "No sign do We abrogate or cause to be forgotten, but that We bring that which is better than it or like unto it."[68] It should also be noted that the language of the Qur'an, according to widespread opinion, does not permit any connotations that are unambiguous to the human mind:

> In the Muslim concept of revelation, the ambiguity of the Qur'an is recognised and emphasised. No human being, not even the Prophet himself, can presume to understand every verse perfectly. Since Muhammad is not considered the author, but rather the medium and at the same time the first recipient of the message sent by God, it is logical that he could not always grasp the richness of meaning of the verses at once. His own words, carefully separated from those received as revelation, are the first and, for all the interpretive competence that belongs to him as a prophet, fallible interpretation of the text, not the commentary of its author. Hence the open-endedness of revelation, its mysteriousness, is not a theological dilemma, but

---

65 On this, see Waardenburg, Jacques, *Islam. Historical, Social, and Political Perspectives*, Berlin / New York: Walter de Gruyter, 2002, 46 ff. ("The Qur'anic Concept of Reason"), esp. 48 f.

66 On this, see Uhde, Bernhard, "'Denn Gott ist die Wahrheit' (Koran 22, 62). Notizen zum Verständnis von 'Wahrheit' in der religiösen Welt des Islam," *Jahrbuch für Religionsphilosophie* 4 (2005), 83 ff.

67 An example of abrogations is the doctrine of the prohibition of drinking grape wine. Praised as a "goodly provision" in Qur'an 16:67, it becomes a concrete prohibition in Qur'an 4:43 ("Draw not near unto prayer when you are drunken") and a general prohibition in Qur'an 5:90 ("Wine [. . .] a means of defilement, of Satan's doing. So avoid it!"). On the problem of abrogation in Qur'an cf. van Ess, Josef, *Theologie und Gesellschaft im 2. und 3. Jahrhundert Hidschra. Eine Geschichte des religiösen Denkens im frühen Islam*, vol. 1, Berlin / New York: Walter de Gruyter, 1991, 34 f.

68 Qur'an 2:106.

> a necessary implication of a message whose sender is God. "If man were given a thousand insights for each letter in the Qur'an, he would not come to the end of the thoughts God has put into one verse of His Book," said the mystic Sahl at-Tustarī (d. 896). "For it is the word of God. But His word is His attribute." And as-Sarrāǧ (d. 988), quoting this statement, adds: "As there is no end with God, so there is no end with the understanding of His Book."[69]

And as-Sarrāǧ continues: "People understand only according to the understanding that God has made accessible to the heart of His friends for His Word. God's word is uncreated. Therefore, the understanding of men comes to no end with it [i.e. God's word] in understanding; for it [i.e. the understanding] came into being and was created."[70] This consideration does not mean that the Qur'an conveys merely an inner knowledge, obscured by the external sense of the word,[71] as mystical poetry suggests:

> There is an outer form to the Qur'an,
> Its inner is more powerful though, good man,
> And inside that there's even a third layer –
> All intellects would lose themselves in there.
> The fourth layer inside none have seen at all
> But God, Who's peerless and incomparable,
> So don't look at its outer form that way –
> The Devil saw in Adam naught but clay.
> The outer form is just like Adam's person,
> That's visible although his spirit's hidden . . .[72]

Although the Qur'an does not allow for a complete understanding, it allows a progressive penetration into its contents. This communication[73] succeeds in a form

69 Kermani, Navid, *Gott ist schön. Das ästhetische Erleben des Koran,* Munich: C.H. Beck, ^{3}2007, 131. Translation by the editor.

70 Sarrāǧ, Abū Naṣr ʿAbdallāh Ibn ʿAlī, *Schlaglichter über das Sufitum: Abū Naṣr as- Sarrāǧs Kitāb al-lumaʿ, eingeleitet, übersetzt und kommentiert von Richard Gramlich,* Freiburger Islamstudien 13, Stuttgart: F. Steiner, 1990, 133.

71 Cf. also Muḥammad al-Ġazzālī's confrontation with the Bāṭiniyya school; on this, see Katona, Tobias, *Vernünftiger Glaube – gläubige Vernunft: eine christliche Anfrage an das Verhältnis von Glauben und Vernunft im Islam,* PhD Thesis, Freiburg 2021, 120 ff.

72 Rūmī, Jalāl al-Dīn, *Masnavi* III, 4247–4251. Trans. J. Mojaddedi, Oxford: Oxford University Press, 2013, 257.

73 On the Qur'an as communication, see Khorchide, Mouhanad, *Gottes falsche Anwälte. Der Verrat am Islam,* Freiburg: Herder, 2021, 188: "The Qur'an is [. . .] a medium of communication between God and human beings – but not only for the first addressees of the Qur'an, it also represents an offer of communication and a promise of relationship to all human beings, precisely in this consists its universal claim." Regarding this, see Abu Zaid, Nasr Hamid, "Der Koran. Gott und Mensch in Kommunikation," in: id., *Gottes Menschenwort. Für ein humanistisches Verständnis des Koran,* ed. Thomas Hildebrandt, Freiburg: Herder, 2008, 122 ff.; Çaviş, Fatima, *Den*

that makes an anagogical understanding of the Qur'an possible; for this purpose, parables also serve for understanding (e.g. Qur'an 29:44) and for exhortation (e.g. Qur'an 39:29).

But how is the human understanding, the human ability to judge, evaluated in contrast to the Qur'anic revelation? Is the human understanding at all capable of judging God's Revelation and the principles of faith when God Himself, exalted above creation and man, is nevertheless "nearer to him [i.e. man] than his jugular vein" (Qur'an 50:16)? The Qur'anic address to human understanding presupposes human understanding, human intellect, but:

> The message of the Qur'an, however, is aestheticised, embedded in and interwoven with the images and parables. Sober reason cannot suffice for the act of understanding. The rational approach to the whole is based on an illusion of logocentrism. For reality cannot be fully comprehended with reason, especially not where language is at work. Language cannot be rationally controlled and mastered because it is, in itself, semantically indeterminate (and ultimately insufficient), so that, according to Derrida, deconstruction decisively rejects the totalitarian gesture of reason. It is not we who dispose of the Qur'an, but vice versa. [. . .] For the Qur'an, in principle, cannot be fully understood, since it is considered to be the Word, the essential act of God. While Hans-Georg Gadamer's hermeneutic concept assumes that understanding is fundamentally possible, the Qur'an, as Jacques Derrida understands it, shows that the Other remains fundamentally the Other in his radical otherness. Here lies the real meaning of what it means when the Qur'an in the Islamic self-understanding is considered a revelation, a sending down of God, so that a "merging of horizons" in the act of understanding with the eternal remains categorically impossible. The divine reality that is present in the Qur'an is not made to disappear, but its otherness, which impossible to be acquired, is preserved, the impossibility of complete understanding, in the sense of a "limited reason" (Günter Figal, Der Sinn des Verstehens. Beiträge zu hermeneutischen Philosophie, Stuttgart 1996, p. 12), endured, the difference guarded and borne.[74]

The language of God, even put into human language, remains unfathomable to the understanding, because the understanding alone is not the instrument to accept and assimilate the Qur'an. This position was also disputed; a deep rift in Islamic theology and intellectual history was made here by the direction of the Mu'tazila, as can already be seen in its co-founder Wāṣil b. 'Aṭā' (c. 699–748): "The missionary movement steered by Wāṣil appealed to people's rational insight, not, as some Sufi movements with similar intentions later did, to their feelings."[75]

Koran verstehen lernen. Perspektiven für die hermeneutisch-theologische Grundlegung einer subjektorientierten und kontextbezogenen Korandidaktik, Paderborn: Schöningh, 2021, 122 ff.

74 Karimi, *Licht über Licht*, 787 f. Trans. by the editor.

75 Van Ess, Josef, *Theologie und Gesellschaft im 2. und 3. Jahrhundert Hidschra. Eine Geschichte des religiösen Denkens im frühen Islam*, vol. 2, Berlin / New York: Walter de Gruyter, 1992, 276.

Under these conditions, a concept of soul (*nafs*) in the Qur'an as a unified doctrine is difficult to discern: "The Qur'an does not contain a doctrine of soul in the strict sense . . .",[76] and "*Nafs* and *Rūh* are used very frequently and in different meanings in the Qur'an . . ."[77] Therefore, even the scheme of abrogation cannot be applied. Thus, it can be concluded: "In view of these specifications, it is not surprising that the Isl. theologians do not develop a unified doctrine on the S."[78] So is there a "concept of the soul" in the Qur'an, in Islam?[79]

The Qur'an often mentions the "soul" (*nafs*).[80] With the different meanings of *nafs*, the Qur'an takes up the different traditions as they have come down from Judaism, the various schools of Greek philosophy, and Christianity. These traditions are presented as different non-contradictory aspects of the "soul". All these aspects consider the soul as self-movement, either in connection with the body or detached from this connection.

From the Jewish tradition, the Qur'an adopts the notion that *nafs* denotes the whole person, the connection of body and soul. Thus, the whole, self-moving person is designated. So, it says: "'Come! Let us call upon our sons and your sons, our women and your women, ourselves and yourselves (*anfusa-nā wa-anfusa-kum*) . . .'"[81] From one soul (*nafs*) God created mankind: "O mankind! Reverence your Lord, Who created you from a single soul",[82] from "a single soul (*nafs*)" he created the persons man and woman,[83] it is this single soul that makes up the living human being as a whole. It is, therefore, also the soul that is called to account for man's deeds after his death, on the "Day of Resurrection":[84] "Whosoever is rightly guided, it is for the sake of his own soul."[85] The soul created by God is immortal, eternally it will dwell in hell[86] or in the gardens of paradise.[87] But this also means that it embraces the whole human being even in his post-resurrection, transformed physicality.

76 Rudolph, Ulrich, "Seele. Islam," in: *RGG*, vol. 7, Tübingen: Mohr Siebeck, 2004, 1095.

77 Stieglecker, *Die Glaubenslehren des Islam*, 688.

78 Rudolph, "Seele. Islam," 1095.

79 Cf. esp. the survey by Elleisy, Magdy, *Die Seele im Islam. Zwischen Theologie und Philosophie*, Hamburg: disserta Verlag, 2013; also Talaat, Sia, *Die Seelenlehre des Korans (unter besonderer Berücksichtigung der Terminologie)*, Halle (Saale): Buchdruckerei H. John, 1929.

80 The word is mentioned 276 times.

81 Qur'an 3:61.

82 Qur'an 4:1.

83 Qur'an 7:189; cf. Qur'an 39:6.

84 Qur'an 39:67.

85 Qur'an 39:41.

86 Qur'an 39:72.

87 Qur'an 39:73.

From the Greek tradition, the neo-Platonic aftermath of Plato's philosophy, it is taken up that the term *nafs* also refers to the spiritual, incorporeal part of the human being, his "inner being". Thus, Jesus speaks to God: "Thou knowest what is in my self (*fī nafsī*), and I know not what is in Thy Self."[88] This one form of the "inner being" – this is also reminiscent of Aristotle's doctrine of the soul – appears in various states whose contents can also be understood as a sequence of stages. The Qur'an names these three states of the soul, incorporating parts of the philosophical tradition as well as aspects of the Christian tradition:

- The "commanding soul" (*an-nafs al-ammāra*). Here reference is made to the Qur'anic passage: "But I absolve not my own soul. Surely the soul commands to evil, save whom my Lord may show mercy."[89] This state of the soul, which in this state can also be called the "appetitive soul",[90] leads to the lower drive, to evil. This assessment is reminiscent of Plato's doctrine of the soul, who wanted the "covetous" (*epithymētikón*)[91] part of the soul, which aims at evil,[92] to be controlled. Thus, the Qur'an takes up the tradition of the philosophical doctrine of the soul.
- The "blaming soul" (*an-nafs al-lawwāma*). Here reference is made to the Qur'anic passage: "I swear by the Day of Resurrection. And I swear by the blaming soul!"[93] This state of the soul refers to the soul "that repentantly laments"[94] on the Day of Resurrection over its failures to overcome its own covetous self:

> The expression [*lawwām*], unique in the Qur'an, could be a reminiscence of the similarly eschatological prediction in Matt 22:13–14, where a wedding parable is used to evoke the judgment in which the unprepared for the feast will be banished to a place of "weeping and gnashing of teeth".[95]

In this regard, the hadith says: "There is no pious or corrupt soul that does not rebuke itself on the Day of Resurrection; if it has done good, it says: 'How have I not done more!' And when it has done evil, it says, 'Would that I had refrained!'"[96] But the self-blaming, repentant complaining soul is to urge the turning away from desires of the "commanding soul", to conversion and repentance, while the person is

---

88 Qur'an 5:116.

89 Qur'an 12:53.

90 Esp. in Mysticism; cf. Gramlich, Richard, *Die schiitischen Derwischorden Persiens. Zweiter Teil: Glaube und Lehre,* Wiesbaden: Franz Steiner, 1976, 66 f.

91 Cf. Plato, *Politeia* 580 e 2 f.

92 Cf. Plato, *Phaidros* 246 b 1 f.

93 Qur'an 75:1–2.

94 Cf. Neuwirth, Angelika, *Der Koran,* vol. 1: *Frühmekkanische Suren*, Berlin: Insel, 2011, 316.

95 Neuwirth, *Der Koran,* vol. 1: *Frühmekkanische Suren*, 420. Trans. by the editor.

96 Tirmiḏī, Nr.2403.

still alive. This is reminiscent of the Gospel as well as Christian theology, for Cyprian says: "Do penance in full, prove the sorrow that proceeds from an aching and lamenting soul."[97]

- The "tranquillised soul" (*an-nafs al-muṭma'inna*). Here reference is made to the Qur'anic passage: "O thou soul at peace! Return unto thy Lord, content, contenting. Enter among My servants. Enter My Garden."[98] This state of the soul denotes the soul which, by the call of God Himself, has returned perfectly at peace to God who fashioned it: "by the soul and the One Who fashioned it."[99] It has attained perfect nearness to God. Here it no longer needs self-movement, here all movement is suspended in pure presence. This recalls the Psalm verse, "With God alone my soul is at rest . . ."[100] and the famous words of Augustine: "inquietum est cor nostrum, donec requiescat in te."[101] The Qur'an takes up these traditions insofar as it refers to the tranquillity of the soul, which, however, is not "in God" but "with God" – as in the Psalm – because God is above additions.

In addition to other states of the soul, the traditional literature adds the "persuading soul" (*an-nafs al-mulhima*). Here reference is made to the Qur'anic passage: "Your souls have seduced you in this matter."[102] This state of soul denotes the transition from the "commanding soul" to the "blaming soul", in that in this state man keeps oscillating between sin and repentance, delaying repentance even as he seeks the state of goodness, but is repeatedly seduced by the persuasions of the "commanding soul", which tends towards evil.[103] This is reminiscent of the Jewish doctrine of the two drives *Yetser ha-tov* ("drive to good") and *Yetser ha-ra* ("drive to evil"); between the two drives it is up to the free will of man to decide and to take responsibility for this decision.[104]

While the pre-Islamic traditions understand the concept of the soul in different ways, the Qur'an seeks to understand these different understandings as predicates of

---

97 Cyprian, *De Lapsis* 32.
98 Qur'an 89:27–30.
99 Qur'an 91:7.
100 Ps 62:1.
101 Augustine, *Confessiones* I,1.
102 Qur'an 12:18; 12:83.
103 Cf. Abū-Ṭālib al-Makkī, Muḥammad Ibn-Alī, *Die Nahrung der Herzen. Abū Ṭālib al-Makkīs* Qūt al-qulūb, *eingeleitet, übersetzt und kommentiert von Richard Gramlich*, vol. 1, part 1–31, Freiburger Islamstudien 16, Stuttgart: Steiner, 1992, 51. On this book "Qūt al-qulūb", see footnote 150.
104 Cf. Grözinger, Karl Erich, *Jüdisches Denken. Theologie-Philosophie-Mystik*, vol. 1: *Vom Gott Abrahams zum Gott des Aristoteles*, Frankfurt a. M.: Campus, 2004, 274 f.

the soul, i.e. to understand the carrier of these predicates uniformly as "soul" (*nafs*). This possibility arises from the correspondence of these predicates, which all presuppose self-movement in the respective predicates. Thus, the "commanding soul" shows the self-movement of the will, often as the drive to evil, the "blaming soul" the self-movement of reflection by referring to itself, the "tranquillised soul" the completed and, thus, abandoned self-movement towards rest with God.

What is significant here is that the states of the soul that the Qur'an attributes to the soul do not form a contradiction, since they do not exist at the same time; also, the regard in which they are ascribed to the soul can be perceived as different. Thus, the states designated by predicates do not fall under the rule of the "law of non-contradiction", as formulated by Aristotle,[105] and can, therefore, be comprehended by the understanding, that understanding which is repeatedly addressed in the Qur'an.

At the death of the human body, this soul detaches itself from the body.[106] This death is certain: "Wheresoever you may be, death will overtake you, though you should be in towers raised high."[107] Through death, God returns the body to the earth from which He took it, to be followed by resurrection and judgement: "From it [i.e. earth] We created you, and unto it We shall bring you back, and from it We shall bring you forth another time."[108] God said to Adam: "In the sweat of thy face only shalt thou eat bread, till thou return unto the earth: for from it thou art taken: for from the earth thou art, and unto the earth shalt thou return."[109] The renewed bringing forth, the raising of the dead – sometimes also understood as the awakening of the mortal soul with reference to the Qur'an verse, "Unto Him [i.e. God] is your [i.e. mankind's] return altogether; God's Promise is true. Verily He originates creation, then He brings it back, that He may recompense with justice those who believe and perform righteous deeds"[110] – leads

105 See footnote 21.

106 Cf. Yusuf, Hamza, "Death, dying, and the afterlife in the Quran," in: Seyyed Hossein Nasr (ed.), *The Study Quran. A New Translation and Commentary*, New York: Harper Collins, 2016, 1819 ff.; van Ess, Josef, *Theologie und Gesellschaft im 2. und 3. Jahrhundert Hidschra. Eine Geschichte des religiösen Denkens im frühen Islam*, vol. 4, Berlin / New York: Walter de Gruyter, 1997, 521.

107 Qur'an 4:78.

108 Qur'an 20:55.

109 Gen 3:19.

110 Qur'an 10:4. Thus taught Abū l-Huḏail (d. 841/227?), cf. van Ess, Josef, *Theologie und Gesellschaft im 2. und 3. Jahrhundert Hidschra. Eine Geschichte des religiösen Denkens im frühen Islam*, vol. 3, Berlin / New York: Walter de Gruyter, 1992, 255. On Abū l-Huḏail cf. ibid., 209–296.

back to God and to His judgement, the compensation of justice: "Say: 'The Angel of death, who has been entrusted with you, will take you; then unto your Lord shall you be returned.'"[111] For "Truly We give life to the dead and record that which they have sent forth and that which they have left behind."[112]

Thus, the soul awaits mercy and justice from God: "Nay, whosoever earns evil and is surrounded by his sins, it is they who are the inhabitants of the Fire, therein to abide. And those who believe and perform righteous deeds, it is they who are the inhabitants of the Garden, therein to abide."[113] The delights of the Garden of Paradise are described – several times in the Qur'an – here as an image, a parable: "The parable of the Garden that has been promised to the reverent: therein lie rivers of water incorruptible, rivers of milk whose flavor does not change, rivers of wine delicious for those who imbibe, and rivers of purified honey. Therein they partake of every fruit and of forgiveness from their Lord."[114] For thus says God to the God-fearing, "O My servants! No fear shall be upon you this Day; nor shall it be you who grieve, you who believed in Our signs and who were submitters; enter the Garden, you and your spouses, made joyous. For them are brought round trays and goblets of gold. Therein is whatsoever souls desire and eyes find pleasing."[115] This "image of the Garden" is contrasted with the descriptions of Hell, "streams of water, milk, wine, and honey" correspond to "a boiling liquid and a cold, murky fluid" as drinks:[116] "Truly, the tree of Zaqqūm is the food of the sinner, like molten lead boiling in their bellies, like the boiling of boiling liquid."[117]

The immortality of the soul is a consequence of its self-movement and the possibility of being separated from the body, so that it can continue its self-movement even if the body has died, i.e. lost its principle of self-movement that gave it life, in order to receive it again with the resurrection by God. The Qur'an only hints at the "interim" between the death of the body and its resurrection, referring to those "who are averse to what God has sent down:" "Then how will it be when the angels seize them, striking their faces and their backs? That is because they followed that which angers God and were averse to His Good Pleasure."[118] The idea of the angels Munkar and Nakīr questioning the dead in the

111 Qur'an 32:11.
112 Qur'an 36:12.
113 Qur'an 2:81–82.
114 Qur'an 47:15.
115 Qur'an 43:68–71.
116 Qur'an 38:57.
117 Qur'an 44:43–46.
118 Qur'an 47:27–28.

grave is not found in the Qur'an, it goes back to traditional literature; "the names of the two angels are mentioned in Tirmiḏī Sunan, ǧanā'iz 70."[119]

It is not easy to distinguish between the terms *nafs* and *rūḥ*: "it should be noted that some theologians distinguish *nafs* and *rūh* as different things, but according to the teachings of the earlier theologians, the two words mean one and the same."[120] Yet: "The term *rūḥ* is known to play a somewhat complex role in the Qur'an (cf. Th. O'Shaughnessy, The Development of the Meaning of the Spirit in the Qur'ān, Rome 1953). But it is never primarily the soul or the breath of life of man that is meant, but the Spirit of God, which at most, as in the conception of Mary, can be breathed into a man."[121] Because this spirit is God's own spirit – spirit is breathed into man "by My Spirit"[122] –, little knowledge of this spirit is given to human knowledge: "They ask thee about the Spirit. Say, 'The Spirit is from the Command of my Lord, and you have not been given knowledge, save a little.'"[123] If the spirit belongs to God, its knowledge exceeds independent human knowledge. Therefore, it is said: "One said to Ibrāhīm an-Naẓẓām: 'What is the most amazing thing in this world?' He replied, 'The spirit (rūḥ).'"[124] At the same time, this Spirit also gives some people a potential that transcends human knowledge, which is found in Jesus[125] and Muhammad,[126] but also in the faith of believers.[127] But this spirit is breathed into human beings and it is distinguished from the soul, which indwellingly harms the divine purity of the spirit, as a later text explains:

> The first contentment that comes before love [of God] is the standing point of trusting God, and the state of the beloved lover is the corresponding state. The second contentment, which comes after love, is the state of knowledge, and the state of the God-trusting lover is the corresponding state. Love is one of the noblest states. Above it there is only the station of friendship (*ḫulla*). This is a standing point of special knowledge. It is the penetration into the secrets of the transcendental, so that man gains insight into the vision of the beloved, insofar as it is granted to him to grasp something of his knowledge of his will, according to his unchanging will and his beginningless, unchanging nature [. . .]. But this is covered by

119 Gramlich, *Stufen zur Gottesliebe*, 365.
120 Stieglecker, *Die Glaubenslehren des Islam*, 688.
121 Van Ess, *Theologie und Gesellschaft*, vol. 3, 246n19.
122 Qur'an 15:28.
123 Qur'an 17:85.
124 Ǧāḥiẓ, *Kitāb al-Ḥayawān* VII, 203, 2; cited in van Ess, Josef, *Theologie und Gesellschaft im 2. und 3. Jahrhundert Hidschra. Eine Geschichte des religiösen Denkens im frühen Islam*, vol. 6, Berlin / New York: Walter de Gruyter, 1995, 112.
125 Cf. Qur'an 4:171.
126 Cf. Qur'an 42:52.
127 Cf. Qur'an 58:22; 16:102.

the imaginative powers of the heart through its intellect and veiled in the hidden depths of the invisible through its spirit. But when the soul exits the spirit like the night out of the day, so that it becomes spiritual (*rūḥānī*), then the afflicted breathes a sigh of relief, and when the mind is unchained from the heart so that it becomes divine (*rabbānī*), the afflictions are dispersed. Thus says the knower (*ramal*):

By my life, O thou my life!
  Do not reject what I do to draw near!
Drive out the soul from the spirit
  And bring refreshment to my sorrows!

And the best of speakers spoke: *And they encompass nothing of His Knowledge, save what He wills.* (Sura 2:255)[128]

The spirit is not the "soul" that is connected to the body. It is handed down from the Mu'tazilites: "Others taught: The self (*nafs*) is something (*ma'nā*) other than the spirit and the spirit again something other than life . . .".[129] What the Qur'an means in a veiled way with regard to the "spirit" becomes clearer in the tradition with regard to the "soul", especially in concrete statements in the literature on piety, and, thus, also in theology.

4 The Concept of "Soul" in Piety and Theology

The "concept of soul" is clear in the Qur'an. The traditional concepts of soul are understood as states of the one soul and as such are ordered into a gradual path. The Qur'anic revelation and then the Islamic tradition begin this path with the soul commanding evil, and so the struggle against this soul is the starting point of the soul's movement towards God. This movement sees the soul first also connected to the body and its desires, to this world, a here and now that is without lasting value, because: "Know that the life of this world is but play, diversion, ornament, mutual boasting among you, and vying for increase in property and children – the likeness of a rain whose vegetation impresses the farmers; then it withers such as that you see it turn yellow; then it becomes chaff."[130] Thus, this

128 Abū-Ṭālib al-Makkī, Muḥammad Ibn-Alī, *Die Nahrung der Herzen: Abū Ṭālib al-Makkīs Qūt al-qulūb, eingeleitet, übers. und kommentiert von Richard Gramlich*, vol. 2, part 32, Freiburger Islamstudien 16, Stuttgart: Steiner, 1992, 583. Trans. by the editor.
129 Aš'arī, Abū l-Ḥasan, *Maqālāt al-islāmīyīn* 337, 4 f., cited in van Ess, Josef, *Theologie und Gesellschaft im 2. und 3. Jahrhundert Hidschra. Eine Geschichte des religiösen Denkens im frühen Islam*, vol. 5, Berlin / New York: Walter de Gruyter, 1993, 428.
130 Qur'an 57:20.

world deserves blame.[131] And, thus, the soul, as long as attached to this world, becomes an enemy.[132] Hence, it is handed down:

> Wuhayb (b. al-Ward) al-Makkī said: I have heard that Jesus said: You disciples! I have brought down this world for you. Do not raise it up again! There is nothing good in a house where one sins against God. Nothing good is in a house if you can only reach the hereafter by leaving it. Pass through it and cherish it not! And know that the root of all sin is the love of this world. Many a covetousness has brought long sorrow to the covetous.[133]

This corresponds to Jesus' word with regard to this world: "The love of this world is deadly. It is the root of all sins. Jesus said, 'The deadliest of all sins is the love of this world.'"[134] The inferior value of this world, which the Qur'an calls "but play, diversion, ornament, mutual boasting",[135] and the love – especially the love of the soul – of this world as the root of all sins "is confirmed by the well-known Holy Report: 'The love of this world is the root of all sins.' For it is the foundation of sin [. . .]. In the reports about Adam we were told: After Adam had eaten of the tree, his stomach stirred for the defecation. But no food of paradise was created to cause this except this tree. Therefore, he was forbidden to eat of it. As he began to walk about in Paradise, God gave an angel a command, addressing him and saying: 'Ask him what he wants!' Adam replied: 'I want to put down the rubbish that is in my belly.' It was said to the angel: 'Ask him: where do you want to put it? On the cushions? Or on the beds? Or in the shadows of the trees? Do you know a place here that is suitable for this? But go down to this world!' God dealt graciously with him and lowered him to the earth."[136]

Thus, this world is like a "privy that is full".[137] This world (*dunyā*) "stinks, but even more stinks a heart that God has afflicted with love of the world."[138] Therefore, the soul's love for the world is a turning towards the repulsive. This love of the "commanding soul" is also a self-contradiction and, therefore, of corruption, a state of soul that must be overcome, as the Qur'anic view of the states of the soul teaches. For it is a self-contradiction to love this world and not God: "It is no sign of love if you love what your beloved hates. Our Lord rebuked the world, we

---

131 Cf. Gramlich, Richard, *Weltverzicht. Grundlagen und Weisen islamischer Askese*, Wiesbaden: Harrassowitz, 1997, 103 ff. ("Der Tadel des Diesseits").

132 Cf. Gramlich, *Weltverzicht*, 178 ff. ("Die Seele als Feind").

133 Dīnawarī, *Al-muǧālasa* 148, 22–25; cited in Gramlich, *Weltverzicht*, 357 f. Trans. by the editor.

134 Abū Nu'aym, *Ḥilyat al-awliyā' wa-ṭabaqāt al-asfiyā'* 8. 145, 8; cited in Gramlich, *Weltverzicht*, 357.

135 Qur'an 57:20.

136 Makkī, *Nahrung der Herzen*, vol. 2, 241.

137 Šiblī, in as-Sulamī, *Ṭabaqāt* 341, 8; cited in Gramlich, *Die schiitischen Derwischorden*, 41.

138 Abū al-'Abbās al-Qaṣṣāb, in 'Aṭṭār, *Taḏkira* 2, 185, 18–19; cited in Gramlich, *Die schiitischen Derwischorden*, 40.

praised it; he hated it, we loved it."[139] And so God said to a prophet, "If you love me, remove the love of the world from your heart, for the love of it and of me do not go together."[140] This view repeats what is encountered in Christian tradition when Jesus speaks, "No one can serve two masters: Either he will hate the one and love the other, or he will be attached to the one and despise the other. You cannot serve God and mammon."[141] And this self-contradiction becomes even clearer in the words, "He that wants be the friend of the world will be the enemy of God."[142]

Precisely this tradition is taken up by pointing out the contradiction that exists between love of the world and love of God. In this context, Qur'anic teaching attributes love of the world, of the evil of this world, to a state of soul that can be abandoned through repentance, by calling this state of soul to account:

> ʿUmar b. al-Ḫaṭṭāb said: "Demand an account of your soul before an account is demanded of you, and weigh it before you are weighed, and adorn yourselves for the great display before God. *That Day you shall be exposed; no secret of yours shall be hidden* (Sura 69:18). The reckoning in the Hereafter will be easy for people who have reckoned with their souls in this world, and the scales of people who have weighed their souls in this world will be heavy in the Hereafter."[143]

Nevertheless, this world is also intended for use. The prophet's words have been handed down: "God gives this world so that it may lead to the hereafter; he does not want to give the hereafter so that it may lead to this world."[144] Life in this world is like a journey: "The world is a sea, the hereafter is a shore, the ship is piety, and men are a travelling company."[145] First of all, an image is taken up here that is also found in the Christian tradition:

> Suppose we were travellers who could live happily only in our homeland, and because our absence made us unhappy we wished to put an end to our misery and return to our homeland: we would need transport by land or sea which we could use to travel to our homeland, the object of our enjoyment. But if we were fascinated by the delights of the journey and the actual travelling, we would be perversely enjoying things that we should be using; and we would be reluctant to finish our journey quickly, being ensnared in the wrong kind of pleasure and estranged from the homeland whose pleasures could make us happy. So in

139 Ibrāhīm b. Adham; cited in Gramlich, *Die schiitischen Derwischorden*, 40n167.
140 Abū Saʿīd b. Abī al-Ḫayr; cited in Gramlich, *Die schiitischen Derwischorden*, 41n167.
141 Matt 6:24.
142 Jas 4:4.
143 Makkī, *Die Nahrung der Herzen*, vol. 1, 272.
144 Cf. Gramlich, *Die schiitischen Derwirschorden*, 42n184.
145 Sulamī, Ṭabaqāt 380, 2; cited in Gramlich, *Die schiitischen Derwischorden*, 42.

this mortal life we are like travellers away from our Lord: if we wish to return to the homeland where we can be happy we must use this world, not enjoy it . . .[146]

The Islamic interpretation of this journey, however, adds an essential explanatory moment to the distinction between this world, which is for use, and the hereafter or God, who alone is for enjoyment. This journey is a journey from the soul turned towards the world, the "commanding soul", towards God: "Al-Ğunayd said: 'The journey from this world to the hereafter is convenient for the believers. Leaving people on the side of God is difficult. The journey from the soul to God is hard and difficult.'"[147] This is explained as follows:

The journey from this world to the hereafter is comfortable and easy for the believer (though there is a certain difficulty in it, since man has to part with what is dear to him – his children and the like. The reason is the perfect reward. For God has promised it to him who renounces this world's lusts, as He said: *as for one who [. . .] forbids the soul from caprice, truly the Garden is the refuge* (Sura 79:40–41). So, it is comfortable and easy in view of what follows). Leaving man on the side of God (that is, in obedience to Him) is difficult (because he must resist the soul's desire – its lusts and their worldly satisfactions). The journey from the soul (by disobeying its desire) to God (by acting for the sake of His mere command) is hard and difficult (because of the aforementioned resistance).[148]

This soul journey corresponds to a journey that begins with the lowest state of soul, the "commanding soul", and ends with the "tranquillised soul". Thus, the sequence of the states of the soul desired by God is an itinerary, a path, a journey from one state of the soul to the next. The identity of the soul consists in its self-movement, its impermanence, its restlessness, until it is transformed into the tranquillised soul, "inasmuch as it was created restless, but rest was commanded to it."[149] Testimony to this from the piety literature and to other aspects of the soul can be found in the famous work *Qūt al-qulūb* ("The Food of Hearts")[150] of Abū Ṭālib Muḥammad

146 Augustine, *De doctrina christiana* I,4. Trans. R. P. H. Green, Oxford: Clarendon Press, 15–17.

147 Gramlich, *Stufen zur Gottesliebe*, 172.

148 Gramlich, *Stufen zur Gottesliebe*, 172: "The probable source is *Qušayrī, Risāla* 85, 3–6, *bāb aṣ-ṣabr*. Text (with Zakarīya al-Anṣārī's commentary in parentheses)."

149 Makkī, *Nahrung der Herzen*, vol. 1, 299.

150 On this book Gramlich comments: "Makkī's Book is first and foremost a book of instruction on the duties of the Muslim and the many forms of Muslim piety, and a guide to a life of conscientious striving for the ideals of religious inwardness. Until the end of the 5th/11th century, it remained the most important and comprehensive work of its kind. However, it was never popular among scholars and pious people in the form that Makkī gave it. This happened only after it had undergone a metamorphosis proper and appeared in the new, more accessible guise of Muḥammad al-Ġazzālī's much-praised magnum opus *Iḥyā' 'ulūm ad-dīn*. *Iḥyā'* is basically nothing more than a reworking of *Qūt*, which takes the material and shortens or expands it as needed, arranges it systematically, formulates it more clearly and presents it in easier-to-understand

b. ʿAlī b. ʿAṭīya al-Ḥāriṯī al-ʿAǧami al-Makkī al-Wāʿiẓ (d. 996/386). The impermanence of the soul, its insatiability, can be seen in its love for this world, the starting point of the soul's journey:

> The description of the soul can be summed up in two terms: impermanence (*ṭayš*) and insatiability (*šaraḥ*). Impermanence comes from ignorance, insatiability from greed. Both are a natural disposition of the soul. With regard to its inconstancy, it is like a ball or a nut that is artificially at rest on a smooth, inclined surface. If you only touch it with your finger and set it in motion a little, it moves by its own nature, namely its lightness and roundness. With regard to its insatiability, which comes from greed, it is like a moth, which, unintelligent and greedy, falls into the fire, because it seeks the brightness with its lack of understanding, but finds its downfall in it. When it has reached a certain brightness, it is not content with little of it because of its insatiability. Greedily it seeks the utmost of it, it seeks the source of brightness and wants all of it. But that is precisely the lamp, and so it burns. If it had come far away in only a little light, it would have remained whole. Such is the soul in its inconstancy, from which comes alacrity, and in its insatiability, from which comes desire. Greed and desire, however, were the two that lead to Adam's expulsion from Paradise. For he had a desire for immortality and was therefore greedy for food. This was on account of lack of understanding and insatiability. Disobedience was the reason for the population of this world, and obedience became the reason for the population of the hereafter. That is why it is said, "The love of this world is the beginning of all sin."[151]

Makkī explains the states of the soul mentioned in the Qur'an in connection with repentance. The four states of the soul – in reverse order in Makkī – are explained as follows:

1. The tranquillised soul

> Then, with regard to repentance, there are four kinds of people. Of each kind there is a group, and each group has a standing point. There is among them (first) one who repents of sin and remains on the straight course in repentance. As long as he lives, he does not persuade his soul to sin again. He exchanges his evil deeds for his righteous good works. This is he who is foremost in good deeds (Sura 35:32), and this is sincere repentance.
>
> *O you who believe! Repent unto God with sincere repentance!* (Sura 66:8).

language, corrects it here and there, and occasionally supplemented from other sources. [. . .] The brittle matter of Makkī's enormous knowledge was given by Ġazzālī a luminous, illuminating form imbued with the grace of the spirit. [. . .] Thus, Makkī's work was transformed into a masterly textbook that is still widely regarded as the greatest creation of the Islamic mind." (Makkī, Nahrung der Herzen, vol. 1, 19) The classification of the work in the realm of "piety" is confirmed by Gramlich, Richard, *Die Lebensweise der Könige. Adab al-Mulūk. Ein Handbuch zur islamischen Mystik. Eingeleitet, übersetzt und kommentiert von Richard Gramlich*, Stuttgart: Franz Steiner, 1993, 1: "With Makkī's *Qūt al-qulūb*, which is more a great encyclopaedia of Islamic piety than an actual Sufi work . . .".

151 Makkī, *Nahrung der Herzen*, vol. 1, 297. Trans. by the editor.

The soul of the human being is the tranquillised, well-liked.

> *O thou soul at peace! Return unto thy Lord, content, contenting.* (Sura 89:27–28).

The Holy Narrative that has come down to us about such a one says: "Go forth! Those who have separated themselves from God's remembrance have won the race. The remembrance of God has lifted the burdens (of their sins) from them, so that they reach the resurrection lightly laden."

The Prophet's word according to Abū Hurayra and Abū ad-Dardā'.[152]

2. The blaming soul

The one who joins this regarding closeness to God is (secondly) a person who is determined to repent and intends to stay on the straight course. He does not pursue sin and does not have it in mind. But sometimes sins overtake him without his intending them, and he is afflicted by occasional lusts and offences. These are characteristics of the believer. For him the straight course is to be hoped for, since he is on its path. He is among those about whom God has said: *Those who shun grave sins and indecencies save what is slight; truly your Lord is of vast forgiveness* (Sura 53:32). To him applies the description of the God-fearing of whom God said: *And who, when they commit an indecency or wrong themselves, remember God* etc. (Sura 3:135). The soul of this man is the blaming one by whom God has sworn

> *I swear by the Day of Resurrection. And I swear by the blaming soul.* (Sura 75:1–2). [. . .]

In the case of such a person, what the traditional Ḥadīṯ[153] says is true: "The believer constantly falls into temptation and always turns back."[154]

3. The persuading soul

The third – he is close to this second in state – is a man who sins, then repents, then sins again, then grieves over it, wanting and seeking sin and preferring it to obedience. He, however, delays repentance, but takes it upon himself to walk in the straight course, and loves the ranks of the repentant, and his heart finds pleasure in the stands of the arch-righteous, whereas the favourable opportunity does not present itself, and his stand does not prevail, because desire presses him, habit irritates him, and indifference overflows him. But between the sins he repents, but he relapses again as a result of the preceding habit. The repentance of this man is an interval from one time to another. For such a man one may hope for the straight course, because he has done good works and these wipe out the evil he had done before, but one must nevertheless fear with him that he will change, because his sinning continues. The soul of this man is the persuading one.

---

152 Makkī, *Nahrung der Herzen*, vol. 2, 49 (insertions by the original translator). Trans. by the editor.

153 Makkī, *Nahrung der Herzen*, vol. 2, 36: "Weak prophet's word handed down by Ali. Aḥmad b. Hanbal, *Al-musnad* 1,80/2,39, Nr 605".

154 Makkī, *Nahrung der Herzen*, vol. 2, 49 f. (Insertions by the original translator). Trans. by the editor.

Your souls have seduced you in this matter. (Sura 12:18; 12:83).[155]

4. The commanding soul

> The fourth servant is the one whose condition is the worst, who has the worst calamity weighing on his soul and who is given the least by God, a person who sins and then follows it up with a similar or greater sin and remains permanently hardened, intending to sin whenever he can. He does not intend to repent, does not intend to keep a straight course, does not hope, thinking well of God, for a promise, and does not fear anything threatened, because he feels quite secure. This is the realisation of impenitence and a stand in presumption and arrogance. About such a one the Holy Report is delivered: "The hardened go straight to their destruction in hellfire." The soul of this man is the one that commands (evil),
>
> *Surely the soul commands to evil.* (Sura 12:53).
>
> and his spirit constantly flees from the good.[156]

These explanations refer to the Qur'an, but with the descriptions of the signs of the respective state of the soul, they give concrete indications of how to recognise this state. This self-knowledge refers to a knowledge in this world, to a path of conversion in this world. "This world" belongs to the "world of earth", "to the world of visibility":

> Know: This world belongs to the world of earth and the world of visibility, the hereafter to the world of the super-sensible and the world of beings. By this world I understand your state before death, by the hereafter your state after death. Your this side and your beyond are, thus, your qualities and states, of which that which is adjacent and near is called this side, that which comes later is called beyond. We are now speaking of the hereafter from this world, we are therefore speaking now in this world, the world of earth, but we have in view the explanation of the hereafter, the world of beings. But it is unthinkable that one could explain the world of beings in the earthly world in any other way than through parables. Therefore, God said: *These are the parables; We set them forth for mankind. But none understand them, save those who know* (Sura 29:43). For the earthly world is asleep in relation to the world of beings. That is why the Prophet said: "People sleep. When they die, they wake up." What will be in the waking state can only be known to you in sleep through the coinage of parables that require interpretation.[157]

"Parables" that impart knowledge in the "world of visibility" explain the invisible or even the otherworldly through the visible. "God is the Light of the heavens and

155 Makkī, *Nahrung der Herzen*, vol. 2, 51 (Insertions by the original translator). Trans. by the editor.
156 Makkī, *Nahrung der Herzen*, vol. 2, 51 f. (insertions by the original translator). Trans. by the editor.
157 Gramlich, *Stufen zur Gottesliebe*, 62 f. On the discourse on the "world to come" in Judaism, see Stemberger, Günter, *Jüdische Religion*, Munich: C.H. Beck, 1995, 109 f.

the earth. The parable of His Light is a niche, wherein is a lamp."[158] Thus, begins the "verse of light". A parable![159] The "garden" (of paradise) is also spoken of in a figure of speech, a parable,[160] for God coins parables:[161] "Truly God is not ashamed to set forth a parable of a gnat or something smaller."[162] The parables also serve as a reminder: "And indeed We have set forth for mankind in this Quran every kind of parable, that haply they may remember!"[163] The parables illuminate what appears dark to man, they open his eyes, as it were, to that which is beyond human knowledge: "The Messenger of God said: 'God said: 'I have prepared for My righteous servants that which no eye has seen, and no ear has heard, and never entered into the imagination of man as the desire of his heart.''"[164] This illumination is necessary, for: "Are the blind and the seer equal, or are darkness and light equal?"[165]

Thus, Makkī also seeks to make the states of the soul, its respective qualities, accessible to knowledge in a kind of parable, of comparison:

> Know: Women have the qualities of the soul. He who knows the qualities of the soul knows through them the qualities of women, and he who knows the qualities of women and has endured them in what he has lived and experienced, thereby knows the qualities of the soul. Among them there are the persuasive (*musawwila*); these are the meanest. And there are the commanding ones (*ammāra*), which are the worst. They tirelessly cause trouble, and they do not cease in their bad behaviour and evil speeches. Others are like the blaming (*lawwāma*) soul. They are righteous women. Others are tranquillised (*muṭma'inna*). These are the righteous, good, calm, contented ones. In short, if a person's salvation of heart and alignment of state lies in celibacy, then I put nothing on the same level as being alone.[166] The least one has in it is salvation. But being saved is a distinction and a gain in this day and age. But if his soul longs to marry and he is not safe from the impulses of lust, let him marry if it is for the good of his religion. If a man has not enough with one wife, let him take another, and if he does not attain his profit and perfect condition and protection by the two, let him take a third, up to four. If the soul is eager for sexual intercourse and its impulse is strong, the women, if changed, have the same function as one, and if one is enough and one does not need more, it replaces four. Thus, God willed to have the form of the soul in the plan according to which he formed it, and thus he distinguished the natures in the idea

158 Qur'an 24:35.
159 On this, see Karimi, *Licht über Licht,* 784 ff.
160 Cf. Qur'an 47:15.
161 Cf. Qur'an 16:75; cf. 22:73.
162 Qur'an 2:26.
163 Qur'an 39:27.
164 Buḫārī, Abū 'Abdallāh Muḥammad b. Ismā'īl, *al-Ǧāmi' aṣ-ṣaḥīḥ*, Nr. 3244.
165 Qur'an 13:16.
166 Cf. the words of the mystic, Abū Bakr aš-Šiblī: "Keep to being alone, blot out your name among people and turn your face to the wall until you die!"; cited in Gramlich, Richard, *Alte Vorbilder des Sufitums. Erster Teil: Scheiche des Westens*, Wiesbaden: Harrassowitz, 1995, 603. Also: "People looking at people is a temptation. To abstain from it leads to the way of God." Ibid. Trans. by the editor.

> according to which he created them. It is said: God has permitted to have four wives at the same time, because there are four natures, one for each nature, corresponding to this own movement and the desire of the soul connected with it . . .[167]

These four qualities are states of a single soul and its "desires". There is no contradiction here, because according to the respective desire of the soul, the respect changes. The knowledge of the four states of the soul allows a ranking of these states:

> God has established three conditions in connection with the wife. If these are fulfilled, then what is sufficient for the man is thereby achieved, and his soul finds rest. This is one of God's signs that point to him. If the three conditions are not fulfilled with a wife, he can add more to her until there are four. These (then) have the same function as one, because (with one) the prerequisites are missing under which God has proclaimed the rest of the soul. But with four women the conditions in the heart of the believers are absolutely fulfilled, just as God has proclaimed. This, too, is one of God's signs and wise dispositions that point to Him. God said: *And among His signs is that He created mates for you from among yourselves, that you might find rest in them, and He established affection and mercy between you* (Sura 30:21). So, if a man finds rest of soul, goodness of heart and love of wife in a single spouse, that is a sign from God, and she is his sufficient and adequate measure. But if he finds rest, goodness, and love only in four, then these are his sufficient measure and possession. God bestows sufficiency and possession (cf. Sura 53:48). He bestows sufficiency with one and gives possession with four . . .[168]

In the parable, this ranking becomes clear. The "tranquillity of the soul", the tranquillised soul, is like the love of a single wife: "If, therefore, a man finds tranquillity of soul, goodness of heart, and love of wife in a single spouse, this is a sign of God, and she is his sufficient and sufficient measure." This state of soul, this love for a single wife, is a "sign of God", is, thus, the highest of the states of soul. This state is a parable of the soul's love for the one God, hence a "sign of God". Thus, the love of woman, of women, is created and desired by God (Qur'an 30:21), and, hence, the Prophet also loved women: "Sahl b. 'Abdallāh said: 'To renounce women is not right, for they had become dear to the Lord of the renouncers.'"[169] This is confirmed by the Prophet's saying, "Beloved to me of this world are women and perfume. And my eyebright is in ritual prayer."[170] Thus, this love, this state of the soul,

---

167 Makkī, *Nahrung der Herzen,* vol. 3, 555 f. It goes without saying that this comparison, even understood in the context of the times, does not correspond to the esteem in which women are held in Islam. An example of a more recent interpretation of the appreciation of women: Idriz, Benjamin, *Der Koran und die Frauen. Ein Imam erklärt vergessene Seiten des Islam,* Gütersloh: Gütersloher Verlagshaus, [2]2019.

168 Makkī, *Nahrung der Herzen,* vol. 3, 557 .

169 Makkī, *Nahrung der Herzen,* vol. 2, 278.

170 Aḥmad b. Ḥanbal, *al-Musnad* 3, 128.

is the transition from the moving soul attached to various desires to the rest of the soul.

The invisible soul, connected with the body, designates the total personality of the human being, consequently also the states of the human being as a body, which are influenced by the soul. The states are an expression of the soul's self-movement, but also an expression of its changeability, with which it deceives man: "How many a man thinks he detests sins, while he cannot commit them, but when he can then find ways and means to do so, without anything disturbing him and without having to fear people, he commits them! If the soul, thus, deceives in forbidden things, beware of trusting its promise in permitted things."[171] The soul, thus, "is a deceiver, *surely the soul commands to evil* (Sura 12:53) and claims to be good."[172] This soul knows no measure, it is insatiable, as a comparison, a parable, makes clear:

> One person has compared the soul, in terms of its insatiability, to a fly that passes by a loaf of bread with honey on it. It sits on it and wants to have it all. But it gets caught with its wing and the honey kills it. Another one then passes by, approaches some of it, takes what it needs, and retreats in one piece.[173]

Therefore, the soul is an obstacle to the love of God, because in its changeableness and insatiability it is always in motion, turned towards this world, until the state where it finds rest with God, expressed in the parable by rest with a woman. Therefore, God is said to have given David what he obtains who keeps away from this world:

> This is a rank which only he attains who rejects this world and his own and does not occupy himself with it with any thought, whose heart is free for me and who has chosen me before all my creation. If it is so, I incline towards him and make his soul free and pull back the curtain between me and him, so that he can look at me like one who looks at something with his eye. Then I always show him my nobility and let him come near to the light of my countenance. When he is sick, I nurse him like a loving mother nurses her child; and when he is thirsty, I give him drink and give him the taste of the thought of me. When I do this to him, David, I make his soul blind to this world and to his own, and do not let it become dear to him, while he occupies himself with me without ceasing.[174]

Thus, this soul, with its states turned towards this world, is not only to be rebuked in regard to these states, but moreover, its desires and urges are to be removed for the attainment of the best state of soul, closeness to and rest with

171 Muhammad al-Ġazzālī in Gramlich, *Stufen zur Gottesliebe*, 459.
172 Gramlich, *Stufen zur Gottesliebe*, 599.
173 Makkī, *Nahrung der Herzen*, vol. 1, 298. Trans. by the editor.
174 Gramlich, *Stufen zur Gottesliebe*, 688. Trans. by the editor.

and love from God, as God says: "David, keep my word! Take away from your soul for your own sake, and let nothing be given to you from it, for otherwise I will shut off my love from you! [. . .] David, make yourself dear to me by being at enmity with your soul! Bar her the way to her lusts, and I will look upon thee, and thou shalt see that the veils between thee and me are taken away! I deal lovingly with you . . ."[175]

The soul, in its connection to the body, is the field in which renunciation is to be practised, renunciation of this world to which the soul is turned. In this regard, see the "Prophet's word transmitted by Abū Idrīs al-Ḫawlīnī from Abū Ḏarr: 'Renunciation of this world does not consist in declaring the permissible as forbidden and wasting one's good. Rather, renunciation of this world consists in not relying more on what is in your hands than on what is in God's hands, and in your desire for the reward of misfortune, when it befalls you, being stronger than for it to have failed to befall you.'"[176] The reward consists in the gain of the soul's nearness to God, a gain already in this world, the transitoriness of which appears obvious to the reflecting mind, because clinging to the transient is a self-contradiction:

> *Thus does God make clear unto you the verses, that happily you may reflect upon this world and the Hereafter* (Sura 2:219; 2:266). That is, would you reflect on the passing away of this world and its transience and on the continuance of the Hereafter and its imperishability and choose the abiding, imperishable and prefer it to the transient, passing away and renounce it. For whose end is vanishing, his end is like his beginning, but his beginning was non-being. But whose end is continuance, he has, as it were, always been, and his beginning is like his end in continuance. Therefore, said the All-Knowing, All-Wise: *While the Hereafter is better and more enduring* (Sura 87:17). [. . .] Man who is blinded by this world and does not know its end is like a silkworm. It keeps spinning threads around itself until it kills itself. It wants to get out, but finds no way out for itself and thus perishes in its own fabric. Her work and toil was for others to enjoy. This is the fate of those who accumulate money and goods for their heirs. They have the enjoyment of it, he has the misery of it. They enjoy it after him, and he perishes through it before them.[177]

Thus, the mind, instructed by the parable, already recognises that the soul's clinging to this transitory world is self-contradictory, and this clinging consists in "labour and toil", while the "renouncer does not rejoice over a transitory happiness of the soul which he has, and is not saddened by not having something of it."[178]

---

175 Gramlich, *Stufen zur Gottesliebe*, 689 f.

176 Tirmiḏī, Muḥammad, *Al-Ǧāmi'* 4, 571, nr. 2340, *zuhd* 29; cited in Makkī, *Nahrung der Herzen*, vol. 2, 279.

177 Makkī, *Nahrung der Herzen*, vol. 2, 239. Trans. by the editor.

178 Makkī, *Nahrung der Herzen*, vol. 2, 227.

Renunciation, then, is "not obeying the desire for pleasure and, by denying this for the soul, selling the soul to the Lord. The gift received in return for this is paradise."[179]

It is unanimously clear to Islamic piety and early theology that the immaterial soul must detach itself from its first state, the movement existing in the turning to this world, because this world represents an antithesis to the hereafter: this world seduces to ever further striving restlessness, the hereafter gives rest, this world is transient, the hereafter endures. In relation to the hereafter, it is even worthless. The concept of the soul is recognisable from a concept that represents in a parable the journey of the soul. The soul is connected with the body, with this world, as the principle of the self-movement of the living, as long as both live in this world, but also after the death of the body during the interrogation in the grave:

> Man should be convinced of the questioning by (the grave angels) Munkar and Nakir and that man is intact in his grave, in possession of body and spirit. They question him about the Unity Creed and about the Messengership. This is the last temptation that comes to the believer, and these two are the tempters of the grave. This is how it was delivered to us by the Messenger of God. This is the meaning of God's Word: *God makes firm those who believe* – it was said: in the questioning by Munkar and Nakir – *with firm speech in the life of his world and in the Hereafter. And God leads the wrongdoers astray; God does whatsoever He wills* (Sura 14:27). The punishment in the grave is truth, wisdom and righteousness in body, mind and soul, which, as they sin together, so they are punished together. And if there is blessedness, it is in body, spirit, and soul, who, as they obey together, so also are blessed together. These are the destinies of the hereafter, which proceed according to the course of Omnipotence, not according to the order of that which is accessible to thought and the habit of the understanding.[180]

It is beyond understanding how, after the death of the body, after the interrogation in the grave, body, soul, and spirit can be "together", for a knowledge of unity remains beyond the reflective mind, it is the knowledge of God, the knowledge "according to the course of omnipotence". Here all human categories are transcended, for "in omnipotence there is no spatiality, no succession, no distance, no temporality."[181]

A knowledge that seeks and finds presence with the oneness, the oneness of God, beyond knowledge of the intellect, is the knowledge of mysticism. Also in Islam. This knowledge grasps what is understood as "soul" in the Qur'an, piety and theology in intensified form and content.

---

179 Makkī, *Nahrung der Herzen*, vol. 2, 222.
180 Makkī, *Nahrung der Herzen*, vol. 3, 145. Trans. by the editor.
181 Makkī, *Nahrung der Herzen*, vol. 3, 145.

5 The Struggle against the "Soul": Mysticism

One of the difficulties regarding the presentation of Islamic mysticism is this fact: "There is no Islamic word for what we call mysticism."[182] This raises the question of whether phenomena of such related content can be encountered outside the Christian occidental tradition, which uses the word "mysticism" derived from the ancient Greek language, that they too can be considered with the word "mysticism".

The word "mysticism", derived from the Greek language, has an original meaning that can be rendered by the English word "to blink". And originally this "blinking" may have meant the squinting of the eyes when they seek to recognise a dimly shining object in darkness in nightly initiation ceremonies, as in Eleusis at the "Mysteries". These "Mysteries", especially ceremonies dedicated to the goddess of grain, "Demeter", consisted, among other things, of a ritual visualisation of the grain sunk into the earth as a death from which new life awakens. Therefore, the Greek word "Mysterion", Latin "Mysterium", used in the sense of a figure of speech, means something "hidden", an "inner meaning". This applies, for example, to the "Theologia mystica" in the interpretation of the Holy Scriptures in Christianity, as an important and tradition-shaping work by Pseudo-Dionysios Areopagita, a teacher writing under this name, is called. And finally, the word "mysticism" is used to refer to those paths that are meant to lead to God hidden from the mind, to attain an immediate presence with God, a presence beyond the knowledge of the mind, a presence with and a presence in "his" unity.

On the question of the transmissibility of the word "mysticism", Annemarie Schimmel noted in her work, "How Universal is Mysticism?":[183] "Mysticism: what is it? Is it the great stream that flows through all religions? Or is it a vain attempt by people to escape so-called reality, to take refuge in a dream world and close their eyes to everyday problems? After all, does the word come from the Greek *myein*, to close one's eyes? Is it, as Coventry Patmore[184] suggests, the knowledge of ultimate principles? And if so, are mystical movements, such as we find in the world's various religious systems, the same, or would it be necessary to invent a different name for each?"[185]

The term "mysticism" can be defined, even if it encompasses various related movements. More precisely, "mysticism" can be defined as a path to presence with

182 Meier, Fritz, *Vom Wesen der islamischen Mystik*, Basel: B. Schwabe, 1943, 7.
183 Schimmel, Annemarie, *Wie universal ist die Mystik? Die Seelenreise in den großen Religionen der Welt*, Freiburg: Herder, 1996, 11.
184 Coventry Patmore (1823–1896) was a British poet who was particularly devoted to religious and mystical themes [Ann. B.U.].
185 Schimmel, *Wie universal ist die Mystik*, 11.

a first unified principle, attainable out of this world, beyond all forms of thinking and willing, which always mean a differentiating separation of an "I" as subject and an object. The goal is presence with or fusion or identity with this principle.

For mysticism in Judaism, Christianity, and Islam, the thought of Plotinus is of fundamental importance. Plotinus knew his teachers.[186] He knew what question the teachers who had made Greek and Roman philosophy significant for all areas of human life were pursuing, and he takes this question and answers it in a new way that creates an epoch: "What is the First Principle of certain knowledge?" And because Plotinus knows these teachers, he also knows the First Principles as they have prevailed in traditional Greek philosophy since the "Metaphysics" of Aristotle, whose text he studied:[187] the "law of non-contradiction" as a formal principle[188] and the reflection of thought as a substantive principle.[189] For Aristotle, both principles are necessary first prerequisites of all thinking and judgement. Plotinus, however, sees: the principles of the traditional epoch are not without presuppositions, i.e. they are not first principles, because they are not completely uniform, for the "law of non-contradiction" examines a problem of assignment, i.e. minimally a duality of subject and predicate, or else the contradiction of the two contradictory predicates, when it excludes the possibility of contradictory predicates being assigned to a subject at the same time and in the same respect. And the "reflection of thinking" also splits into thinking and thought, which think each other: and so here, too, a minimal duality is set, which in turn presupposes the concept of "unity".[190] This "unity" is now "beyond", "beyond" all two-ness and all being that always collapses into multiplicity.[191] And so this "unity" would be unknown to man, since it is beyond, if it had not lowered itself into thinking and the individual soul and, thus, founded the thought of the necessity of its presupposition.[192] The necessity of the presupposition of this "unity" is, therefore, understandable, but not this unity itself; Plotinus shows: the "otherworldly" unity is not temporal and not local as a unity, and yet it is the cause of everything and the goal of everything:

> But the First beyond being does not think: Intellect is the real beings, and there is movement here and rest. The First itself is not related to anything, but the other things are related to it,

---

186 Cf. Plotinus, *Enneads* V, 1,8 ff.
187 Cf. Porphyry, *Life of Plotinus 14, 6 f.*
188 Cf. Aristotle, *Metaphysics* 1005 b 5 ff.
189 Cf. Aristotle, *Metaphysics* 1072 b 13 ff.
190 Cf. Plotinus, *Enneads III, 8,9,1 f.*
191 Cf. Plotinus, *Enneads III, 9,9.*
192 Cf. Plotinus, *Enneads* V, 1 f.

> staying around it in their rest, and moving around it, for movement is desire, but it desires nothing, for what could it desire, it which is the highest?[193]

Thus, this "first", this unity as "God" is the principle for philosophy as well as for theology. But it is also the uniform principle of all human thought and action as the "good",[194] limited neither in time nor in space and the goal of everything, the goal of all virtues.[195] Just as in the triangle the point that unites the catheti at the apex is itself withdrawn from view and yet "holds" the triangle, so this "first", this "unity", in the necessity of its presupposition, works for the entire emerging world, just as in the image Gothic vaults are crowned by the one keystone, just as the one emperor crowns the empire, just as the one pope crowns the Church. From all this arises an order according to a First Principle, an order, of course, that cannot and must not be called into question. Thus, this order is a hold and a deprivation of freedom at the same time.

This designation also captures what in Islamic languages, admittedly, is not designated by a word that could be translated as "mysticism", for the "Muslims named their mystics after a peculiar garb first attested in Kufa in the 8th century, *Ṣūfīs*, 'wool-clad ones', from *ṣūf*, 'wool'. But the name '*Sufism*', *Taṣawwuf*, 'to clothe oneself with wool', in the sense of mysticism, is only applicable to Islamic mysticism. The time for which this name is first attested coincides approximately with the beginnings of the thing designated by it, although we have more exact knowledge of Islamic mysticism only from the ninth century onwards, when Baghdad had become its centre."[196]

The simple "woollen clothing", which cools in summer and warms in winter, has been the sign of the ascetics who existed even before the famous Baghdad mysticism. The ascetics from the city of Baṣra are particularly worthy of mention here, especially Ḥasan al-Baṣrī (642–728 CE). An extra-Qur'anic word of God[197] is attributed to him, which speaks of the mutual "love" between God and man. "Some of his disciples apparently concluded from this that one could already experience paradise on earth. Admittedly, they tried to absolve him of such excesses: when they once let him participate in the apparitions they had in the desert at night, he immediately noticed that the girls of paradise had horses' feet."[198]

---

193 Plotinus, *Enneads* III, 9,9. Trans. A. H. Armstrong, Cambridge, MA / London: Harvard University Press, 1980, 415–417.

194 Cf. Plotinus, *Enneads* III, 9,9, 415–417.

195 Cf. Plotinus, *Enneads* I, 2.

196 Meier, *Vom Wesen der islamischen Mystik*, 7.

197 An "extra-canonical word of God" (*Ḥadīṯ qudsī*) is a tradition that belongs to the collection of prophet's words. Its chain of tradents leads beyond the prophet to God Himself.

198 van Ess, *Theologie und Gesellschaft*, vol. 2, 98.

In the Qur'an, God speaks to believers about people whom "He loves and who love Him."[199] The teaching of the ascetics, whose mysticism seeks to realise the mutual love between God and man,[200] took up a basic theological-philosophical stance of Islam, a basic stance based on the avoidance of self-contradiction in order to proclaim the message of Islam in an understandable way.

Now this attitude is already laid down in the Qur'anic revelation. Man neither can nor should love the world and God, "this world" and "the hereafter", and certainly not love the world more than the hereafter: "Those who prefer the life of this world over the Hereafter, and who turn from the way of God and seek to make it crooked; it is they who are far astray."[201] This applies to all Muslims, but especially to the Sufi, the mystic who seeks presence with God. Therefore, Islamic mysticism has the tendency to despise the world, to get away from it towards God. Basically, the Sufis, the Islamic mystics, see themselves as Muslims who live their faith without compromise, who seek to surrender completely to God, which

---

199 Qur'an 5:54.

200 The talk of mutual 'love' between God and man is a fine example of how translations often cannot reliably reflect what the original expresses and should, therefore, be used with caution only. The Word of God traced back to Ḥasan al-Baṣrī, who uses the word *'išq* (as verbal forms) for this mutual love, not the verbal forms of the word *maḥabba* used in the famous Qur'anic verse 5:54 ("[a people] whom He loves and who loves Him"). Both words are usually translated as "love", but are precisely distinguished by the Islamic mystics. Richard Gramlich comments: "I would like to assume that in the famous text by 'Abd al-Wāḥid b. Zayd (d. 177/793) [and traced back to Ḥasan al-Baṣrī], which speaks of the mutual *'išq* between God and man [. . .], by *'išq* is to be understood neither passion nor infatuation nor [. . .] an increased pleasure, but the unfulfilled love (on the part of man), the love at a painful distance, the unsatisfied desire for love in contrast to the enjoyment of love. Massignon's remark [Louis Massignon, Essai sur les origines du lexique technique de la mystique musulmane. Nouvelle edition. Paris 1954] that 'Abd al-Wāḥid b. Zayd used the words *'išq* and *šawq* ('marquant le désir'), not *maḥabba* ('marquant la consummation'), for the love of God (*Essai*[2] 214), perhaps comes closest to the correct facts. As proof, one could cite that Nūrī wanted the words *maḥabba* and *'išq* to be understood by the theologians in this way. Ġulām Ḫalīl [d. 888; on him cf. van Ess, *Theologie und Gesellschaft*, vol. 4, 281 f.] had accused him because he had said (as it seems to me consciously applying the aforementioned Word of God to himself): I love (*a'šaqu*) God and He loves me (*ya šaqunī*). Nūrī defended himself: 'I heard God say [in the Qur'an]: '[a people] whom He loves and who loves Him' (*yuhibbuhum wa-yuhibbūnah*; Qur'an 5:54). But *'išq* is no more than *maḥabba*, rather the *'āšiq* [lover] is one kept away (*mamnū'*), but the *muhibb* [lover] in the enjoyment of His love.'" Gramlich, *Die schiitischen Derwischorden*, 304f.n1621. This fact is described in such detail because it is easy to see that in one form of "love" distance, i.e. no union, is meant, but in the other form enjoyment of love, i.e. union in love, but in both cases and in this form of mysticism no monism or identity of God and man, as expressed somewhat later in the "theopathic love of God" of a Ḥusayn b. Manṣūr, called Ḥallāǧ (executed 922).

201 Qur'an 14:3.

is the word meaning of "Muslim" (= "someone surrendering [to God]"). Nevertheless, it should be noted:

> Although the Islamic mystics have always tried to bring their movement into line with the Qur'an and the Sunna as far as possible, and strong personalities have emerged both inside and outside Sufism to show it the way again and again, it has never allowed itself to be beaten over a bar. Sufism changed its face from person to person and from group to group as early as the classical period (3rd–5th/9th–11th centuries) and then on through the Middle Ages and modern times. The people involved noticed this themselves and often pointed it out. [. . .] Aḥmad Ẓarrūq (d. 899/1493) philosophises on this: "Never do two men agree on all points about one and the same thing, even if they agreed with each other in the core or in the derivations or in some aspects; that is why it has been said: the ways to God are as numerous as the breaths of the creatures."[202]

And so, a shared aspect is found in Islamic mysticism after all: the rebuke of the soul and the struggle against the soul.[203] Hence, in a Sufi manual on Islamic mysticism, it says at the beginning of the chapter "The Practices of the Sufis":

> The practices (*rusūm*) of the Sufis are: the struggle (*muǧāhada*) against the soul, the renunciation of the pleasures of the senses (*šahawāt*) and the resistance to the desire for pleasure (*hawā*). God said: *But as for those who strive for Us, We shall surely guide them in Our ways* (Sura 29:69). Muǧāhid (b. Gabr) said: 'It is the struggle against the soul (= against oneself).' The Messenger of God was asked, 'Who is a fighter of faith?' He replied, 'Whoever fights against his soul for the sake of God.' It is narrated from al-Ḥasan (al-Baṣrī): 'Once, when people came from the Prophet, he said: 'Welcome! God grant you long life! You have come from the small war of faith to the great war of faith.' They asked, 'Messenger of God, what is the great war of faith?' He replied, 'The man's fight against his soul and his desire for lust for the sake of God.' The Sufis fight against their soul because the soul invites resistance to God and loves that wherein one finds ruin and destruction and is at enmity with God.[204]

202 Meier, Fritz, *Abū Sa'īd Abū l-Ḫayr (357–440/967–1049). Wirklichkeit und Legende,* Acta Iranica 11, Teheran- Liege: E.J. Brill, 1976, 1 f. Trans. by the editor.
203 What Fritz Meier, the eminent expert on Islam and Islamic mysticism, said in the preface to the printed version of his public habilitation lecture, "Vom Wesen der islamischen Mystik" ("On the Essence of Islamic Mysticism") may apply to the following: "One could, however, reproach the author for the fact that he, 'while feeling the spirit of the whole, does not focus enough on the individual, that when others cannot see the forest for the trees, he forgets the trees above the forest'. But what I have offered could only be one of the possible longitudinal sections through the subject [. . .]. I have, therefore, confined myself to depicting the main feature that jumps out at me the most and to taking this depiction as far as possible into depth." Cf. Meier, *Wesen der islamischen Mystik,* Prologue.
204 Gramlich, Richard, *Die Lebensweise der Könige. Adab al-Mulūk. Ein Handbuch zur islamischen Mystik. Eingeleitet, übersetzt und kommentiert von Richard Gramlich,* Stuttgart: Franz Steiner, 1993, 45. Trans. by the editor.

Here, in enhancement of the practice of faith, the struggle against the soul becomes the "great war of faith". While Islamic piety seeks to accompany and strengthen the soul on its journey to reach its goal in rest, in being at peace with God, Sufi mysticism also knows this journey as the "education" of the soul.[205] In this way, the soul is attributed the potency for good, which has to do with its origin:

> Out of the marriage between spirit and body came the two children heart and soul. The heart is a son who resembles his father, the spirit, and the appetitive soul is a daughter who resembles her earthy mother. In the heart dwell all praiseworthy, heavenly, spiritual qualities, in the soul all blameworthy, earthly, lowly qualities. But since the soul is a child of the spirit, some good qualities connected with the spirit nature also dwell in it.[206]

The union of the spirit, which originates in the hereafter and is turned towards it, with the body on this side, also produces the soul, which is turned towards this side and, as the appetitive soul, resembles its mother, the body. Therefore, piety has the goal of renouncing this world, because this also means renouncing the inclinations of the appetitive soul; the Sufi exaggeration of this thought makes the renunciation of this world appear as a renunciation of the soul through spiritual struggle:

> Spiritual struggle is nothing but opposition to the appetitive soul, and it is basically only a matter of weaning it from its habits and inducing it to permanently oppose its own drives. In the same way, renunciation is directed against the appetitive soul, because one renounces what is pleasurable to it. It consists in wishing away all the lusts of the soul, or in giving up the soul's lusts for everything of this world – especially for possessions, rank, honour, and the praise of men. Although renunciation in the Sufi sense is directed towards this world (*dunyā*), that which distracts from God and is non-divine, it is not the world that is affected by this renunciation, but, just as in the spiritual struggle, one's own soul, which is attached to it and makes things *dunyā* through its attachment to it. That is why Abū Ṭālib al-Makkī concludes that a real renunciation of this world is a renunciation of the soul.[207]

This attitude is in accordance with the Qur'an: "As for one who fears standing before his Lord and forbids the soul from caprice, truly the Garden is the refuge."[208] With this renunciation,[209] the prerequisite for the greater renunciation is given, the renunciation of this world and the hereafter:

---

205 Cf. Gramlich, *Die schiitischen Derwischorden*, 71.

206 Muḥammad Ǧaʿfar-i Maǧḏūbʿalīšāh Kabūdarāhangī, *Marāḥil us-sālikīn* 47, 12–16; cited in Gramlich, *Die schiitischen Derwischorden*, 72.

207 Gramlich, *Die schiitischen Derwischorden*, 287–289. Trans. by the editor.

208 Qur'an 79:40–41.

209 On the "renunciation" cf. Gramlich, *Weltverzicht*, 11 ff. ("Das Diesseits und der Verzicht").

> According to Maḥmūd-i Kāšānī, the renouncer has given up the desire for this world and desires the hereafter, paradise, *therein is, whatsoever souls desire* (Sura 43:71). He still has soulish desire. The Sufi, on the other hand, desires neither this world nor the hereafter. His rank in renunciation is, therefore, higher than that of the "renouncer."[210]

Muḥammad al-Ġazzālī concludes:

> He who spurns everything except God, even the gardens of Paradise, and loves God alone, is a renouncer per se. He who spurns every pleasure [pleasures to which the soul is turned] that can be attained in this world, but does not renounce these similar pleasures in the hereafter, but desires the virgins of Paradise, the castles, the rivers and the fruits, is also a renouncer, only less than the first. He who renounces some comforts of this world but not others, like one who renounces money but not prestige, or who renounces lavish food but does not renounce adorning himself with adornment, does not deserve to be called a renouncer per se.[211]

In this increase of renunciation, every volitional movement of the soul is abandoned, and with it every movement of the soul, which is, nevertheless, self-movement and, thus, life. Therefore, in order to attain this, this soul is to be killed in intensification of the spiritual struggle against the soul: "'Slaughter the appetitive soul!' – this was supposedly the only thing that Abū Sa'īd b. Abī al-Ḫayr had to proclaim in all his speeches."[212] Similarly, the great Sufi sheikh, Abū Naṣr as-Sarrāǧ (d. 988), also wrote in one of the oldest of the extant classical manuals for Sufis, "an indispensable source for the study of the history of Islamic piety in the first centuries [of the Islamic calendar]."[213] This comprehensive work, the "Highlights on Sufism", gives clear guidelines for the theory and practice of Sufism by setting out "the science of Sufism and the teachings of the Sufis".[214] Sarrāǧ cites:

> Abū Sa'īd al-Ḫarrāz said in an instruction to one of his companions: "Heed my instruction, novice! Desire God's reward! But this means that you approach your evil soul and make it dwindle through obedience, leave it, kill it through resistance, slaughter it through despair of the non-divine, kill it through the life of God, and that God is sufficient for you . . ."[215]

A further increase in piety towards Sufi mysticism is the insight that the world,[216] that this world, for which the soul strives, has no value whatsoever, which is why

---

210 Gramlich, *Weltverzicht*, 52. Trans. by the editor.
211 Muhammad al-Ġazzālī in Gramlich, *Stufen zur Gottesliebe*, 456. Trans. by the editor.
212 Gramlich, *Die schiitischen Derwischorden*, 71.
213 Sarrāǧ, *Schlaglichter über das Sufitum*, Introduction.
214 Sarrāǧ, *Schlaglichter über das Sufitum*, 39.
215 Sarrāǧ, *Schlaglichter über das Sufitum*, 385. Trans. by the editor.
216 Cf. Ritter, Hellmut, *Das Meer der Seele. Mensch, Welt und Gott in den Geschichten des Farīduddīn 'Aṭṭār*. Leiden: R.J. Brill, 1955, 45 ff. ("Die Welt").

the renunciation of this world has no object of renunciation. Thus, Abū Yazīd al-Basṭāmī is reported to have said:

> To Abū Mūsā he said: "'Abd ar-Raḥīm, what is he talking about?" I [Abū Mūsā] replied: "About renunciation." He asked, "Of what?" I replied, "Of this world." Then he shook his hand [throwing it away] and said: "I thought he was talking about renouncing something. This world is nothing. What is he renouncing?"[217]

In the highest state of the mystic, the soul is dead, the world is nothing. But this is the renunciation of renunciation, thus the renunciation of the soul determining the I, the renunciation of one's own self:[218]

> Abū Sa'īd b. al-A'rābī said of his Sufi sheikhs: "Renunciation meant for them that this world no longer has any value for the heart, since it is nothing. The renunciant, as far as he is concerned, makes no renunciation because he gives up nothing, since this world is nothing." That – on my life! – is the renunciation of renunciation. For man renounces, but then does not look at his renunciation. He renounces it because he sees nothing, because he renounces a nothing. This is similar to our statement that the real renunciation is the renunciation of the Self. For man can renounce this world for his Self by seeking counter-values for it, so that this is a desire on account of a quality. But when he renounces his Self, for which he wants the counter-values, on the basis of renunciation, then that is the real renunciation.[219]

With this station, the "Self" is freed from the property of the soul and at the same time has itself attained "becoming un-self" (*fanā'*):[220]

> By the becoming un-self is meant the becoming un-self of the quality of the soul and the becoming un-self of the denial and the finding of refreshment through a state that has occurred, but the subsistence says that man remains with it. Further, it is the becoming un-self of man's seeing his own actions in his actions, since God intercedes for him in them, and the subsistence means that man remains in seeing God interceding for him in his intercession for God before he intercedes for God through God.[221]

This "becoming un-self" allows the soul, body, and everything else to sink into God. 'Aṭṭār tells a beautiful parable about this:

---

217 Makkī, *Nahrung der Herzen*, vol. 2, 285.

218 On this, see Uhde, Bernhard, "Ich und Ich-Losigkeit in Mystik und Buddhismus," in: Klaus Brücher (ed.), *Selbstbestimmung. Zur Analyse eines modernen Projekts*, Berlin: Parados, 2015, 124ff.

219 Makkī, *Nahrung der Herzen*, vol. 2, 281. This line of thought resembles Meister Eckhart, Deutsche Predigt 52: "*Beati pauperes spiritu, quoniam ipsorum est regnum caelorum" (Mt 5,3)* – "*Selig sind die Armen im Geiste, denn das Himmelreich ist ihrer.*" Cf. Meister Eckhart, "Deutsche Predigt 52," in: Josef Quint (ed.), *Meister Eckhart. Die deutschen Werke.*, vol. 2: *Predigten*, Stuttgart / Berlin / Cologne: Kohlhammer, 1971, 478–524 and 727–731.

220 On this, see Ritter, *Meer der Seele*, 575 ff. ("Entwerden und Einswerden mit der Gottheit").

221 Sarrāǧ, *Schlaglichter über das Sufitum*, 479.

> A stone and a clod of dirt set out on a journey together. They both fall unawares into the sea. The stone says: I have drowned; now I can tell the bottom of the sea about my experiences. But the earth lump disappears, it escapes into itself. I don't know where it has got to and where it has gone. It speaks in a mute language, but one that is audible to those who know it: "Nothing remains of my body in either world. Neither body nor soul can be seen of me. – If you rise in this sea and disappear in it, you will become a shining pearl in it; if you want to preserve your being, you will attain neither life nor wisdom."[222]

The "sinking" (*istiġrāq*) into the sea ends with the dissolution of the "I" into God, the finite sinks into the infinite – which cannot be limited against the finite without self-contradiction. ʿAṭṭār opposes the idea that sinking into God leads to an identity with God:

> Everyone who becomes Him is a sinking one (*mustaġriq*); far be it from you to say that he is God! If you have become what we have said, you are not God, but you are continually sunk in God.[223]

For ʿAṭṭār, the image of a drop in the sea suggests itself: "Whoever attains the nearness of God for a moment is like a drop of dew in the sea. The drop that sank in the sea, for him both worlds apart from God are only delusion. The water of the sea surrounds him . . ."[224] Here the journey of the soul, of the Self, could end. But even this "high station" is not the final destination. It is followed by the cessation of the becoming un-self to "abide" in God. ʿAṭṭār describes this "abiding": "When one disappears (*az miyān raft*), that is the 'becoming un-self' (*fanā*), when one has withdrawn from this becoming un-self (*fanā gašt az fanā = al fanā' ʿan al-fanā'*), that is 'abiding' (*ḫaqā*). – If you want to reach this high station, first become un-self, but then continue to travel forward out of the nothingness!"[225] Thus, writes ʿIzz ud-dīn Maḥmūd:

> The becoming un-self is the end of the journey to God and the persistence is the beginning of the journey into God. The journey to God ends when one has completely traversed the desert of existence with the step of sincerity, and the journey into God is realised when, after absolute de-emergence, man is given an existence and being purified of the filth of events, so that he thereby ascends into the world of being endowed with the divine qualities and endowed with the moral qualities of God.[226]

Thereby the transition from the non-being of the Self to being in the divine, in God, is accomplished and with it the perfect unity with God: "The hindering Self is cleared away, the hitherto hindered can, without being a second next to God,

222 Ritter, *Das Meer der Seele*, 580 f.
223 Ritter, *Das Meer der Seele*, 590. Trans. by the editor.
224 Ritter, *Das Meer der Seele*, 594.
225 Ritter, *Das Meer der Seele*, 633.
226 Cited in Gramlich, *Die schiitischen Derwischorden*, 261n1369.

be alone with him. Therefore, Šiblī could be heard to say, 'All my life I have desired to be alone with God, without Šiblī being present in that aloneness.'"[227] In this way, the infinite Being of God can fully emerge, which was hidden as a secret in the Self, in the soul (*nafs*): "The Self (*nafs*) holds a secret that God only made known through the tongue of Pharaoh when he said: I am your Supreme Lord."[228]

The journey into God eludes independent human representation; not only does the first journey, the soul's journey to God, end, but words also end, the information reserved for a mission from God. This journey into God is recorded in 'Aṭṭār:

> If I were to speak to you here of this journey, I would certainly throw the two worlds together. If I am given another life, then I will give you an account (*šarḥ*) of it. If I make a new book for this journey, I will fill both worlds with light for all eternity. If I am given permission by divine providence to do so, I am ready. But it would be a mistake if I myself were to give this account. Only then may I do so when I am given permission to do so by the divine royal court. I have given a complete account of this (first) journey; now I must wait for the order to come.[229]

With this, the soul is submerged, completely devoid. This last culmination is the culmination of devotion to God, Islam.

6 A "Concept of the Soul" in Islam?

Early on, Islamic intellectual history produced different perspectives on the "soul" (*nafs*). After the Qur'anic foundations and the tradition literature, and with the emergence of the piety books, treatises of a different kind are found, such as – for example – the medical writing, *Kitāb Maṣāliḥ al-Abdān wa-l-Anfus* ("Book of the Maintenance of the Body and the Soul") by the polymath, Abū Zayd Aḥmad b. Sahl al-Balḫī (850–934). This writing[230] criticises the separation of body and soul and shows their mutual effect on each other. The author devotes the second part of the work to the soul.[231] The state and condition of the soul are discussed in eight sections:

227 'Aṭṭār, *Taḏkira* 2, 165, 5–6; cited in Gramlich, *Die schiitischen Derwischorden*, 325. Trans. by the editor. Cf. Meier, *Abū Saʿīd Abū l-Ḫayr*, 85 ff. ("Der Austausch des Ichs gegen Gott").

228 Gramlich, *Die schiitischen Derwischorden*, 325n1750.

229 'Aṭṭār, *Muṣībatnāme*, End of 40, before the Xātima; cited in Ritter, *Meer der Seele,* 632 f. Trans. by the editor.

230 Cf. Özkan-Rashed, Zahide, *Die Psychosomatische Medizin bei Abū Zaid al-Balḫī. Mit einer Reproduktion der zweiten Abhandlung von Abū Zaid al-Balḫīs Handschrift Maṣāliḥ al-abdān wa-l-anfus in Faksimile.* Düren: Shaker, [4]2019.

231 On this, see Badri, Malik, *Abū Zayd al-Balkhī's Sustenance of the Soul. The cognitive behavior Therapy of a ninth century Physician. Translation and annotation of the ninth century Manuscript*, London: The International Institute for Islamic Thought, 2013.

> The first chapter is composed of an introductory article discussing the importance of sustaining the health of the *nafs* or soul, a synonym to the modern conception of the psyche or mind, but with an Islamic spiritual dimension. Chapter two entitled "Sustenance of Psychological Health" comprises an ultra-modern essay on mental hygiene or preventive mental health. Chapter three is titled "Ways of Regaining Psychological Health When One Loses It." The title of Chapter four is, "Enumerating the Psychological Symptoms and Specifying their Distinguishing Attributes," being the exact translation of the Arabic title, *Dhikr al-A'rādh al-Nafsāniyyah wa Ta'dīdihā.* The Arabic word *a'rādh* is the plural of *'arādh* which is used in modern medicine and psychiatry to represent the English word 'symptom'. Al-Balkhī however uses the term *a'rādh* for both symptoms and disorders. So his usage of the terms *al-A'rādh al-Nafsāniyyah* in the title of the chapter actually means "psychological disorders." The title of Chapter five is, "How to Counteract Anger and Get Rid of It;" Chapter six, "Tranquillizing Fear," (*Taskīn al-Khawf wa al-Faza'*); Chapter seven, "Methods of Dealing with Sadness and Depression," (*Tadbīr Daf' al-Ḥuzn wa al-Jaza'*); and lastly Chapter eight is on "Mental Maneuvers that Fend off the Recurring Whispers of the Heart and the Obsessive Inner Speech of the Soul," (*Fī al-Iḥtiyāl li Daf' Wasāwis al-Ṣadr wa Aḥādīth al- Nafs*).[232]

This psychosomatic study, thus, opens up a different concept for the soul than the theological writings present. This becomes particularly clear when already in the first part of the complete work, which is dedicated to the body, drinking is dealt with in the 6th chapter, "especially the dietetics and ethics of wine consumption":[233]

> As the best and most intelligent product of the human art of preparation (*bi-tadbīrihim wa-'uqūlihim*), the "fine grape juice" (*aš-šarāb al-'inabī ar-raqīq*) is presented, and it is wine that dominates the further sections of the chapter. The beneficial effects of this drink, which has "the noblest substance" (*ašrafuhā ǧawharan*) among all drinks, are enumerated in detail: Only wine benefits both the body and the soul; the body benefits through health and strength, the soul through joy and vivacity; health and joy are the most desirable things in this world for man. Wine is even more likely to strengthen a weak patient than meat, for the effect of wine is much more promptly observed than that of meat: not only does the complexion *(al-alwān)* of the wine drinker change in a very short time, but joy and vivacity, broad-heartedness (*aryaḥiyya*), inner movement (*ihtizāz*), wantless happiness (*ġinā n-nafs*), generosity (*ruḥb aḏ-ḏirā'*), and dissolution of sorrow and sadness immediately set in. Another beneficial effect of wine is the awakening of hidden faculties of the soul, e.g. courage and munificence, but also intellectual faculties such as memory, intelligence, dexterity of tongue, and sharpness of thought – effects, admittedly, that can only be observed in the "middle stage" (*al-ḥāl al-mutawassiṭa*) of wine consumption.[234]

This hymn of praise to the enjoyment of wine, even if it presupposes the medically permitted use of drinking wine, also shows a conception of the soul that is

232 Badri, *Abū Zayd al-Balkhī's Sustenance of the Soul*, 11 f.

233 Biesterfeldt, Hinrich, "Ein Philosoph trinkt Wein," in: Thomas Bauer / Ulrike Stehli-Werbeck (eds.), *Alltagsleben und materielle Kultur in der arabischen Sprache und Literatur. Festschrift für Heinz Grotzfeld zum 70. Geburtstag*, Wiesbaden: Harrassowitz, 2005, 91.

234 Biesterfeldt, "Ein Philosoph trinkt Wein,", 92. Trans. by the editor.

accessible to physical-organic effects. This soul is the immaterial interior of the human being, which, however, not only experiences changes through will, but also through wine, which also extend to the material body. These changing effects are called "beneficent", acting as it were like medicine. In particular, wine causes the "dissolution of sorrow and sadness". Here, an idea is taken up that already finds expression in early Greek poetry,[235] but also in Jewish tradition, as it says: "Give strong drink to those who are perishing, and wine to the afflicted souls, that they may drink and forget their misery and remember their misfortune no more . . ."[236] For it is wine that gladdens the heart of man,[237] and even the Qur'an – in an abrogated passage – praises wine as "goodly provision".[238] The soul, recognisable in the effect of wine, is not separate from the body, but in mutual interrelation, as conveyed by the "secular" Greek tradition and the "religious" Jewish tradition. This gives another aspect of an Islamic concept of soul.

Other aspects are given by the philosophical works, which are guided in particular by the doctrine of the soul of Greek philosophy.[239] It should be noted that Islamic philosophy is supposed to be consistent with the Islamic religion because, as Ibn Rušd puts it, "they are companions by nature and inclined to each other in love, both in essence and in natural disposition."[240] Thus, this philosophy reveals itself as "the inner necessity of the religion of Islam, which demands its explication . . ."[241] Nevertheless, this philosophy also develops its own thoughts on the soul in great abundance,[242] which, however, give an intelligible form that is free of self-contradictions to the Qur'an or piety literature or mysticism. Some thinkers also

---

235 This is reminiscent of the effect of wine which was sung about in ancient Greek poetry: as Homer has previously stated, Odyssey IV, 219 f. it is described that Helena puts a "pharmakon" into a wine that then allows "all evils to be forgotten"; in Alcaeus it is the wine itself that brings this about: "Friend, take down the large decorated cups. The son of Semele and Zeus gave men wine to forget their sorrows." (Alcaeus, Fragment 346, in: Campbell, David A. (ed.), *Greek Lyric 1: Sappho and Alcaeus*, trans. David A. Campbell, Cambridge, MA: Harvard University Press, 1982, 379–381.). On this, see Uhde, Bernhard, "Meerschwein und Messwein. Speisekulte und Kultspeisen – religiös und profan," in: Stephan Loos / Holger Zaborowski (eds.), *"Essen und Trinken ist des Menschen Leben". Zugänge zu einem Grundphänomen*, Freiburg / Munich: Karl Alber, 2007, 128 ff.

236 Prov 31:6–7.

237 Cf. Ps 104:15.

238 Cf. Qur'an 16:67; see footnote 67.

239 Cf. van Ess, *Theologie und Gesellschaft*, vol. 4, 515 f.; Stieglecker, *Glaubenslehren des Islam*, 693 ff.

240 Cited in Karimi, *Licht über Licht*, 147.

241 Karimi, *Licht über Licht*, 148.

242 Cf. Elleisy, *Seele im Islam*.

brought all these sources together in the doctrine of the soul, such as Ṣadr ad-Dīn Muḥammad Shīrāzī, called Mullā Ṣadrā (1571–1640):

> Mulla Sadra believed that his philosophic enterprise strived to provide reasoned arguments for the ideas present within the Qur'an, and the Islamic tradition more generally. He also strived to describe the testimony of the Islamic mystical experience with the same reason-based approach.[243]

This shows that Islam has different concepts of "soul" (*nafs*). However, they agree that the soul, even incorporeal, is in relation to the body, that the soul is self-motion, hence life, that the soul is changeable and is changed on its journey through life to God.

7 Tradition as the Present: The Timelessness of Sources and the History of the Impact of Literature

In the faith and understanding of Islam, the Qur'an is a timeless testimony of God's love for mankind. However, it has to be interpreted again and again in the respective time without changing its original text.[244] In this respect, this text is timeless as the Word of God.[245] But the old sources of piety literature and mysticism also have an effect far beyond their time into the present, which is why they can serve as prerequisites and as testimonies of present interpretations. Thus, Richard Gramlich, in his numerous conversations with dervishes about basic questions of Sufism, was able to state: "Here an old teaching of Islamic mysticism lives on . . ."[246]

An explanation for this understanding of tradition may be found, in all recent theological and philosophical works, in the understanding of history that is to be distinguished from occidental intellectual history. If recent occidental history is characterised by that of the Enlightenment, Islam understands itself, from the

---

243 Shabestari, Mohammad Modjtabed, "What does Mullā Ṣadrā Think about the Soul? A Philosophic Reflection," in: Reza Hajatpour / Maha El Kaisy-Friemuth (eds.), *Ibn Sina and Mulla Sadra. On the Rediscovery of Aristotle and the School of Isfahan*, Freiburg / Munich: Karl Alber, 2021, 100.
244 Cf. e.g. Tamer, Georges, "Alter Wein in neuen Schläuchen? Zum Umgang des Averroes mit dem Qur'an und seiner Rezeption im zeitgenössischen islamischen Denken," in: Wilhelm Schmidt-Biggemann / Georges Tamer (eds.), *Kritische Religionsphilosophie. Eine Gedenkschrift für Friedrich Niewöhner*, Berlin / New York 2010: Walter de Gruyter, 47 ff.
245 See the controversies surrounding Nasr Hamid Abu Zaid's book *Naqd al-ḫiṭāb ad-dīnī* ("Critique of the religious Discourse") in 1992.
246 Gramlich, *Die schiitischen Derwischorden*, 3.

beginning, as a religion of the Enlightenment, in that it sees itself as a religion of the non-self-contradictory mind[247] that sets itself apart from Judaism and Christianity. Thus, a timeless height of form is reached, the content of which is always open to interpretation.

The "concept of soul in Islam", thus, acquires a timeless spectrum of aspects, distinguished by glances from different vantage points. And yet all these glances remain directed towards the highest goal of all devotion, towards the highest goal of what Islam means as devotion to God, for

"unto Him is the final return."[248]

Bibliography

Aristotle, "On the soul," in: id., *On the soul, Parva Naturalia, On Breath*, trans. W.S. Hett, Cambridge, MA / London: Harvard University Press, 1975.

Aristotle, *Metaphysics. Books I-IX*, trans. H. Tredennick, Cambridge, MA / London: Harvard University Press, 1989.

Augustine, *De doctrina christiana*, trans. R. P. H. Green, Oxford: Clarendon Press, 1995.

Badri, Malik, *Abū Zayd al-Balkhī's Sustenance of the Soul. The cognitive behavior Therapy of a ninth century Physician*. Translation and annotation of the ninth century Manuscript, London: The International Institute for Islamic Thought, 2013.

Biesterfeldt, Hinrich, "Ein Philosoph trinkt Wein," in: Thomas Bauer / Ulrike Stehli-Werbeck (eds.), *Alltagsleben und materielle Kultur in der arabischen Sprache und Literatur. Festschrift für Heinz Grotzfeld zum 70. Geburtstag*, Wiesbaden: Harrassowitz, 2005, 89–104.

Campbell, David A. (ed.), *Greek Lyric 1: Sappho and Alcaeus*, trans. David A. Campbell, Cambridge, MA: Harvard University Press, 1982.

Çaviş, Fatima, *Den Koran verstehen lernen. Perspektiven für die hermeneutisch-theologische Grundlegung einer subjektorientierten und kontextbezogenen Korandidaktik*, Paderborn: Schöningh, 2021.

Elleisy, Magdy, *Die Seele im Islam. Zwischen Theologie und Philosophie*, Hamburg: disserta, 2013.

Enders, Markus, "Das Leben als Prinzip der Selbstbewegung – zum Verständnis des Lebens in der Philosophie der Antike, in der christlichen Bibel und der Philosophie des lateinischen Mittelalters," in: Franziska Neufeld / Chiara Pasqualin / Anne Kirstine Rønhede / Sihan Wu (eds.), *Leben in lebendigen Fragen. Zwischen Kontinuität und Pluralität*, Freiburg / Munich: Karl Alber, 2021, 29–70.

van Ess, Josef, *Theologie und Gesellschaft im 2. und 3. Jahrhundert Hidschra. Eine Geschichte des religiösen Denkens im frühen Islam*, 6 vols., Berlin / New York: Walter de Gruyter, 1991–1997.

247 On this, see Uhde, Bernhard, "Christentum und Neuzeit – Neuzeit und Islam? Oder Bedarf der Islam einer Aufklärung? Bemerkungen zu einem Missverständnis," in: Wilhelm Metz / Karlheinz Ruhstorfer (eds.): *Christlichkeit der Neuzeit – Neuzeitlichkeit des Christentums. Zum Verhältnis von freiheitlichem Denken und christlichen Glauben*, Paderborn: Schöningh, 2008, 179 ff.; Karimi, *Licht über Licht.*, 143 ff: "Der Islam als eine Religion des Verstandes".

248 Qur'an 42:15.

Gätje, Helmut, *Studien zur Überlieferung der aristotelischen Psychologie im Islam*, Heidelberg: Winter, 1971.
Gara, Nizar Samir, *Die Rezeption der Philosophie des Aristoteles im Islam: als Beispiel die Rezeption der Seelenlehre des Aristoteles bei Ibn Sīnās Buch ʿIlm al-nafs (Die Wissenschaft der Seele)*, PhD Thesis, Heidelberg, 2003.
Grabmann, Martin, *Die Grundgedanken des heiligen Augustinus über die Seele und Gott*, Darmstadt: Wissenschaftliche Buchgesellschaft, 1967.
Gramlich, Richard, *Die schiitischen Derwischorden Persiens. Zweiter Teil: Glaube und Lehre*, Wiesbaden: Franz Steiner, 1976.
Gramlich, Richard, *Muhammad al-Ġazzālīs Lehre von den Stufen zur Gottesliebe. Die Bücher 31–36 seines Hauptwerkes eingeleitet, übersetzt und kommentiert*, Wiesbaden: Franz Steiner, 1984.
Gramlich, Richard, *Die Lebensweise der Könige. Adab al-Mulūk. Ein Handbuch zur islamischen Mystik. Eingeleitet, übersetzt und kommentiert von Richard Gramlich*, Stuttgart: Franz Steiner, 1993.
Gramlich, Richard, *Alte Vorbilder des Sufitums. Erster Teil: Scheiche des Westens*, Wiesbaden: Harrassowitz, 1995.
Gramlich, Richard, *Weltverzicht. Grundlagen und Weisen islamischer Askese*, Wiesbaden: Harrassowitz, 1997.
Grözinger, Karl Erich, *Jüdisches Denken. Theologie-Philosophie-Mystik*, vol. 1: *Vom Gott Abrahams zum Gott des Aristoteles*, Frankfurt a. M.: Campus, 2004.
Halft, Dennis, "Abrahami(ti)sche Religionen," *Wort und Antwort. Dominikanische Zeitschrift für Glauben und Gesellschaft* 62, 4 (2021), 146–149.
Heckel, Theo K. "Die Seele im hellenistischen Judentum und frühem Christentum," in: Georg Gasser / Josef Quitterer (eds.), *Die Aktualität des Seelenbegriffs. Interdisziplinäre Zugänge*, Paderborn: Schöningh, 2010, 327–342.
Ibn Qayyim al-Ǧawziyya, *Die menschliche Seele*, trans. Alper Soytürk, Fulda: independently published, 2020.
Idriz, Benjamin, *Der Koran und die Frauen. Ein Imam erklärt vergessene Seiten des Islam*, Gütersloh: Gütersloher Verlagshaus, 2019.
Johnson, Aubrey R., *The Vitality of the Individual in the Thought of Ancient Israel*, Cardiff: University of Wales Press, 1949.
Karimi, Ahmad Milad, *Licht über Licht. Dekonstruktion des religiösen Denkens im Islam*, falsafa. Horizonte islamischer Religionsphilosophie 1, Freiburg / Munich: Karl Alber, 2021.
Katona, Tobias, *Vernünftiger Glaube – gläubige Vernunft: eine christliche Anfrage an das Verhältnis von Glauben und Vernunft im Islam*, PhD Thesis, Freiburg 2021.
Kermani, Navid, *Gott ist schön. Das ästhetische Erleben des Koran*, Munich: C.H. Beck, 2007.
Khorchide, Mouhanad, *Gottes falsche Anwälte. Der Verrat am Islam*, Freiburg: Herder, 2021.
Kitzler, Petr, "Nihil enim anima si non corpus. Tertullian und die Körperlichkeit der Seele," *Wiener Studien 122* (2009), 145–169.
Krienke, Markus, *Theologie – Philosophie – Sprache. Einführung in das theologische Denken Antonio Rosminis*, Regensburg: Friedrich Pustet, 2006.
al-Makkī, Muḥammad Ibn-ʿAlī Abū-Ṭālib, *Die Nahrung der Herzen. Abū Ṭālib al-Makkīs* Qūt al-qulūb, *eingeleitet, übersetzt und kommentiert von Richard Gramlich*, 4 vols., Freiburger Islamstudien 16, Stuttgart: Steiner, 1992–1995.
Meier, Fritz, *Vom Wesen der islamischen Mystik*, Basel: B. Schwabe, 1943.
Meier, Fritz, *Abū Saʿīd Abū l-Ḫayr (357–440/967–1049). Wirklichkeit und Legende*, Acta Iranica 11, Tehran / Liege: E.J. Brill, 1976.

Meister Eckhart, Deutsche Predigt 52, in: Quint, Josef (ed.), *Meister Eckhart. Die deutschen Werke*, vol. 2: *Predigten*, Stuttgart / Berlin / Cologne: Kohlhammer, 1971, 478–524; 727–731.
Meyer, Martin F., "Der Wandel des Psyche-Begriffs im frühgriechischen Denken von Homer bis Heraklit," *Archiv für Begriffsgeschichte* 50 (2008), 9–28.
Nasr, Seyyed Hossein (ed.), *The Study Quran. A New Translation and Commentary*, New York: Harper Collins, 2016.
Neuwirth, Angelika, *Der Koran*, vol. 1: *Frühmekkanische Suren*, Berlin: Insel, 2011.
Özkan-Rashed, Zahide, *Die Psychosomatische Medizin bei Abū Zaid al-Balḫī. Mit einer Reproduktion der zweiten Abhandlung von Abū Zaid al-Balḫīs Handschrift Maṣāliḥ al-abdān wa-l-anfus in Faksimil*, Düren: Shaker, 2019.
Plotinus, *Ennead III*, trans. A. H. Armstrong, Cambridge, MA / London: Harvard University Press, 1980.
Ritter, Hellmut, *Das Meer der Seele. Mensch, Welt und Gott in den Geschichten des Farīduddīn 'Aṭṭār*, Leiden: R.J. Brill, 1955.
Rösel, Martin, "Die Geburt der Seele in der Übersetzung: von der hebräischen näfäsch über die psyche der LXX zur deutschen Seele," in: Andreas Wagner (ed.), *Anthropologische Aufbrüche: Alttestamentliche und interdisziplinäre Zugänge zur historischen Anthropologie*, Forschungen zur Religion und Literatur des Alten und Neuen Testaments 232, Göttingen: Vandenhoeck & Ruprecht, 2009, 151–170.
Rudolph, Ulrich, "Seele. Islam," in: *Religion in Geschichte und Gegenwart*, vol. 7, Tübingen: Mohr-Siebeck, 2004, 1095–1096.
Rūmī, Jalāl al-Dīn, *Masnavi III*, trans. J. Mojaddedi, Oxford: Oxford University Press, 2013.
Schimmel, Annemarie, *Wie universal ist die Mystik? Die Seelenreise in den großen Religionen der Welt*, Freiburg: Herder, 1996.
Stemberger, Günter, *Jüdische Religion*, Munich: C.H. Beck, 1995.
Stieglecker, Hermann, *Die Glaubenslehren des Islam, Neuedition der Auflage von 1983. Mit Einleitungen von Petrus Bsteh, Mouhanad Khorchide und Rüdiger Lohlker. Überarbeitung durch Philipp Bruckmayr*, Paderborn: Schöningh, 2021.
As-Sarrāǧ, Abū Naṣr 'Abdallāh Ibn 'Alī, *Schlaglichter über das Sufitum: Abū Naṣr as- Sarrāǧs Kitāb al-luma'*, eingeleitet, übers. und kommentiert von Richard Gramlich, Freiburger Islamstudien 13, Stuttgart: F. Steiner, 1990.
Shabestari, Mohammad Modjtabed, "What does Mullā Ṣadrā Think about the Soul? A Philosophic Reflection," in: Reza Hajatpour / Maha El Kaisy-Friemuth (eds.), *Ibn Sina and Mulla Sadra. On the Rediscovery of Aristotle and the School of Isfahan*, Freiburg / Munich: Karl Alber, 2021, 100–103.
Talaat, Sia, *Die Seelenlehre des Korans (unter besonderer Berücksichtigung der Terminologie*), Halle (Saale): Buchdruckerei H. John, 1929.
Tamer, Georges, "Alter Wein in neuen Schläuchen? Zum Umgang des Averroes mit dem Koran und seiner Rezeption im zeitgenössischen islamischen Denken," in: Wilhelm Schmidt-Biggemann / Georges Tamer (eds.), *Kritische Religionsphilosophie. Eine Gedenkschrift für Friedrich Niewöhner*, Berlin / New York 2010: Walter de Gruyter, 47–83.
Uhde, Bernhard, *Erste Philosophie und menschliche Unfreiheit. Studien zur Geschichte der Ersten Philosophie, Part I*, Wiesbaden: Franz Steiner Verlag, 1976.
Uhde, Bernhard, "PSYCHE – EIN SYMBOL? Zum Verständnis von Leben und Tod im frühgriechischen Denken," in: Gunther Stephenson (ed.), *Leben und Tod in den Religionen. Symbol und Wirklichkeit*, Darmstadt: Wissenschaftliche Buchgesellschaft, 1985, 103–118.
Uhde, Bernhard "'Kein Zwang in der Religion' (Koran 2,256). Zum Problem von Gewaltpotential und Gewalt in den 'monotheistischen' Weltreligionen," *Jahrbuch für Religionsphilosophie* 2 (2003), 69–89.

Uhde, Bernhard, "'Denn Gott ist die Wahrheit' (Koran 22,62). Notizen zum Verständnis von 'Wahrheit' in der religiösen Welt des Islam," *Jahrbuch für Religionsphilosophie* 4 (2005), 83–97.
Uhde, Bernhard, "Meerschwein und Messwein. Speisekulte und Kultspeisen – religiös und profan," in: Stephan Loos / Holger Zaborowski (eds.), "Essen und Trinken ist des Menschen Leben". Zugänge zu einem Grundphänomen, Freiburg / Munich: Verlag Karl Alber, 2007, 128–147.
Uhde, Bernhard, "Christentum und Neuzeit – Neuzeit und Islam? oder Bedarf der Islam einer Aufklärung? Bemerkungen zu einem Missverständnis," in: Wilhelm Metz / Karlheinz Ruhstorfer (eds.): *Christlichkeit der Neuzeit – Neuzeitlichkeit des Christentums. Zum Verhältnis von freiheitlichem Denken und christlichen Glauben*, Paderborn: Schöningh, 2008, 179–191.
Uhde, Bernhard (ed.), *Der Koran*, trans. Ahmad Milad Karimi, Freiburg: Herder, 2009.
Uhde, Bernhard, *Warum sie glauben, was sie glauben. Weltreligionen für Andersgläubige und Nachdenkende*, Freiburg: Herder, 2013.
Uhde, Bernhard, "Ich und Ich-Losigkeit in Mystik und Buddhismus," in: Klaus Brücher (ed.), *Selbstbestimmung. Zur Analyse eines modernen Projekts*, Berlin: Parados, 2015.
Volke, Stefan, *Sprachphysiognomik. Grundlagen einer leibphänomenologischen Beschreibung der Lautwahrnehmung*, Freiburg: Karl Alber, 2007.
Wendt, Reinhard (ed.), *Wege durch Babylon. Missionare, Sprachstudien und interkulturelle Kommunikation*, Tübingen: Narr, 1998.
Waardenburg, Jacques, *Islam. Historical, Social, and Political Perspectives*, Berlin / New York: Walter de Gruyter, 2002.
Yusuf, Hamza, "Death, dying, and the afterlife in the Quran," in: Seyyed Hossein Nasr (ed.), *The Study Quran. A New Translation and Commentary*, New York: Harper Collins, 2016, 1819–1855.
Abu Zaid, Nasr Hamid, "Der Koran. Gott und Mensch in Kommunikation," in: Nasr Hamid Abu Zaid, *Gottes Menschenwort. Für ein humanistisches Verständnis des Koran. Ausgewählt, übersetzt und mit einer Einleitung von Thomas Hildebrandt*, Freiburg: Herder, 2008, 122–158.

Suggestions for Further Reading

Calverley, E.E. / Netton, I.R., "Nafs," in: P. Bearman et. al. (eds.), *Encyclopeadia of Islam*, Second Edition, Leiden / Boston: Brill, 1993.
Kiesel, Dagmar / Ferrari, Cleophea, *Seele*, Erlanger Philosophie-Kolloquium Orient und Okzident 2, Frankfurt a. M.: Klostermann, 2017.

Christoph Böttigheimer and Wenzel M. Widenka

Epilogue

Occidental history of philosophy reflected early about the soul, mainly in connection with the body. Therefore, it is impossible to elaborate the concept of the soul without regard to the concept of the body.

In the history of philosophy mainly dualistic, as well as monistic approaches appeared, when talking about the soul. A dualistic perspective shapes the Platonic tradition. The body is opposed to the soul and downgraded in comparison. The body, as Plato's *Phaidon* reads, is the "prison of the soul". From this prison, the immortal soul has to free herself, to see the truth, or rather the ideas and to return to the world of ideas. Coming from the reception history of Neo-Platonism, the duality of body and soul flows into the Christian tradition and with it the degradation of the body.

Platonic as well as Aristotelic ideas were also incorporated into the Jewish tradition and the Islamic one. So each one of the three religions Judaism, Christianity and Islam holds the soul as immortal. Sura 17:85 reads: "And they ask you, [O Muhammad], about the soul. Say, 'The soul is of the affair of my Lord. And mankind have not been given of knowledge except a little.'" So what conclusion can be drawn from the elaborations given in this volume?

The Concept of Soul in Judaism

The Jewish quest for the human soul offers surprising insights. First of all, we must distinguish between the faith of ancient Israel, when the temple still surmounted Jerusalem, and the Rabbinic time after the Jewish Wars against the Romans, when sacrifices had to stop and the exile began. Speaking of the soul in the time of the Hebrew Bible differs immensely from Rabbinic speculations about the transcendent, immaterial part of the human being. However, the former are the foundation of the latter.

The traces of the human soul in the Hebrew Bible are scarce. In contrast to other near-eastern cultures, Israel shared very little knowledge about the soul. Here a striking feature about the Jewish Religion appears for the first time: its orientation towards life in the here and now. The Hebrew terms for soul, *nefesh*, *ruaḥ* and *neshamah* all allude to respiration and life force. As long as the human body breathes, it is alive. Life force is connected to God's own breath that hovers over the waters of creation. Man is, however, different from animals that have

https://doi.org/10.1515/9783110748239-004

the *ruaḥ*. He acquires a breath of life, *nishmat ḥayyim*, directly from God. Notably though, no matter if it is an animal or a human being, the breath of life, the *ruaḥ* and thereby the life force is situated in the blood of the object of creation. Creatures are composed of a physical body and a wind-like life force that is, however, not to be confused with a philosophical construction we might call a soul. It is neither pre-existent nor immortal. It only exists in combination with a body, so that both parts and their composition define a living creature. Within this framework the abovementioned terms can simply be used to describe someone's personality or simply a person as such, like modern conceptions of the soul often frame the word in psychological terms. Overall, the Hebrew Bible offers nearly nothing that comes close to a transcendental or philosophical understanding of the soul.

This is explainable due to the already mentioned orientation towards this world and the human life span. God is a God of the living, not of the dead. The idea of life after death and individual immortality outside of the family line of inheritance and tradition only arose in later times. There was no need for a soul that pre-existed and continued to exist after death. It is only in times of grief and national disaster, when God's presence and justice seem absent, that speculations about immortality arise. The greatest loss of ancient Judaism is the destruction of its spiritual centre, the Jerusalem Temple, by Roman hands. It is exactly in the aftermath of this moment of desolation and despair that the Rabbis start to shape a conception about the human soul that enables to deal with the heavy burden of a present that lost its orientation. The Rabbis, whose influence dominated Judaism in the 4th–6th century, had to sustain a Judaism that nearly faced its end as a nation. The Temple lay in ruins, the people were scattered over the earth and Christianity was on the rise. The reaction towards the catastrophic events of the near past was twofold: on the one hand, an a-political attitude was adopted in order to avoid direct political confrontation with the surrounding powers. The focus was once again on individual everyday life and the scrupulous fulfilment of the commandments. On the other hand, the Rabbis transcended the urge and hope for liberation and salvation into the world to come, leaving the course of the world to God's hands. Redemption would surely come, one day, but in messianic times. Until then, Judaism turned inwards and became a religion of law and orthopraxy. The soul now had to live on, awaiting judgement and justice, like the world itself longed for redemption. In this paradoxical conception between individual law-abiding and messianic hope, we encounter a more familiar thought about the human soul than it used to be in Biblical times.

Even in the Talmudic period that followed the destruction of the temple, speculations about the immortality of the soul were not yet as sophisticated as they became once the Rabbis took control. The soul now becomes an independent creation and leaves the field of simple respiration. Body and soul are still a necessary unity, none can be complete without the other and Judaism knows no devaluation of the body in contrast to the soul. In Judaism resurrection means resurrection of both the soul and the body and neither of these parts can exist individually, apart from the other. To each soul, there is a corresponding body and both originate in God. Every soul that has ever been and will ever be born was created in advance. Redemption will only come when every single soul that has been created has lived its predestined life with its corresponding body. Thus, the Rabbis found an explanation for the as yet unredeemed world and the hesitation of God's final salvific agency. God has a plan that is in action and man must remain trusting and loyal to his Creator.

The soul, which returns to God after the physical end of its corresponding body in order to wait for the resurrection of both parts, is nothing without the body, it is like a child that does not know the world. It is no better or worse than the body. All depends on man's free decision for good or evil. Interestingly, both the body and the soul are free to choose which inclination to follow, so both can sin and tempt the other part to sinful behaviour. Both the body and the soul will finally face judgement before the throne of the Almighty. This view is elaborated on in several tractates of the Talmud. The Rabbis differ in their opinion whether the soul waits for the body or is rewarded or punished immediately after death. What we encounter here are thoughts about the postmortem entrance into paradise or hell. Rabbinic conceptions of the soul in these times are not consistent; they sometimes end up in speculation and contradiction. Nevertheless, it remains focal that resurrection is always thought of as a *bodily* resurrection.

Medieval Jewish sketches of the soul show a more Platonic approach. Adopting a stream already current among medieval Islamic thought, Judaism developed an image of the immortality of the human soul without falling into the trap of dualism. Competing Aristotelian concepts, e.g. that of Maimonides, denied the existence of an immortal soul and associated immortality with impersonal reason and intellect. In each concept, the everyday behaviour of the Jew, the orientation towards the here and now remains central. The soul never triumphs over the body and vice versa, both remain closely connected. The Middle Ages, however, are the great era of Jewish mystical thought, the Kabbalah, and here the soul claims its rightful throne of independent existence. As there are several layers of existence, of created worlds, connecting immanence with transcendence, the soul climbs several stages of spiritual existence to finally reach its destiny, purified from the foulness of the world. These concepts existed side by side despite their contradictions.

From these unsystematic elaborations emerge all streams of current Jewish thought about the soul. Rabbinic approaches towards the human spirit, soul, whatever it was called, remain central to any elaboration on the subject. From the idea of final divine judgement stems the notion of the pre-creation of all existing souls. Until each pair is united and the world can be redeemed, Jews have to remain faithful to the commandments and to their Creator. Even though times are grim and dire, God's plan is at work and redemption will come. There is no valorisation of one part over the other and there can be no desire for martyrdom, for body and soul are both places and means of worship. Death is not the end. In the meantime, the Jew has to take care of both his body and his soul so that neither may face danger and damage. Both of them are capable of discerning between good and evil and to wisely choose a path.

The Concept of Soul in Christianity

Having lost its heavy influence in recent theological anthropology, the concept of soul is, however, an important object in patristic and medieval Christian theology. It is noteworthy here that the Christian idea of the soul is opposed to Platonic concepts of a soul detached and independent from the body. Christianity believes in the resurrection of both the body and the soul, for both are a gift of God's grace. Man belongs to God, and body and soul are ultimately bound to their creator.

The starting point is what Christianity calls the "Old Testament". Hellenistic speculations about the immortal soul are scarce here; we encounter the biblical concept of the soul as a life force that fills the body like a breath. "Nefesh" is the breath of life with which man is endowed by God's grace. Life therefore ultimately belongs to God; without the breath of life, the creature crumbles back to dust. Man depends on the life-giving relationship to his creator. The Old Testament sees man as the bodily image of God, as the image of a statue; he is not close to the Creator because of his immortal soul. Because of this closeness, man is exalted above all other creatures and able to rule over them. This power to dominate is a result of the divine gift, the breath of life. The biblical scriptures emphasise the unity of body and soul that both constitute the entire human being. It is not an opposition as in Greek philosophy. "Soul", "spirit" and "flesh" are never juxtaposed but denote the whole of human existence. Biblical language is not abstract or metaphysical; it makes use of physical imagery to denote certain qualities of human behaviour. *Nefesh* is not something man possesses, but rather something he is. Its basic meaning is "breathing", not a spiritual desire or connection to the transcendent world. At death, the breath leaves the human body. This breath, this *nefesh*, has marked the individual human being and defines a person as a living being.

When translated into the Christian biblical languages of Greek and Latin, *nefesh* often becomes *psyche* or *anima*, resp. On the other hand, the second most common word for the soul, *ruaḥ*, is often translated as *pneuma* or *spiritus*, which adds a certain bias for reason and ratio and veils the vital aspects of biblical thought. *Ruaḥ* is the wind that once hovered over the waters of creation; it belongs to God and stands for the divine powers man is endowed with by his creator. It is remarkable that Biblical thought does not know a dualistic devaluation of the flesh in contrast to the divine spirit. It is about the whole of creation, about the spiritual-carnal unity that defines a human being. Biblical thought always focuses on the relation of man with his creator, not on a contrast of spiritual und fleshly creation. Both parts of the human being have different relations to God, but they are all the same part of the beloved creation. Nothing God created is regarded as of minor worth, unlike in Greek philosophy. As we have seen above, Biblical thought is oriented towards life itself in the here and now. It is only later that the hope for eternity and the transcendence of earthly life arose. Greek influence is traceable in the later Hellenistic layers of the Old Testament when the "soul" becomes associated with man being an image of his creator.

The apostle Paul adopts these biblical foundations. Man as a whole is determined by sin or grace. However, his use of the biblical *termini* and their translation offers a particular thematic program. He agrees in presenting man as composed of different layers with different connections towards God, but he adds to the layer of "flesh" (*sarx*) the reference to the "original sin". "Spirit" and "flesh" thus become two ways to choose from, but both denote the whole of the human being, not contradictory parts of him. Paul prefers to use the neutral "body" instead of the negatively connoted "flesh" that stands for man's weakness when confronted with the pleasures of this world. He also makes use of the term "soma", which finds no equivalent in the Old Testament and is the most comprehensive of terms used. It is important that Paul favours bodily redemption, not redemption from the body, what would be a Gnostic idea. He follows Old Testament concepts of the inseparable unity of man's body and soul, of what defines a person.

In the New Testament writings, life is also a concept of the relationship between Creator and creature. The term used here, *psyche*, has a broad scope of meanings and cannot be simply translated as "soul". This would ignore the aspects of "life" it encompasses. This is where man and God come into communion. Jesus values human life, as shown in the many healing miracles that explicitly focus on health that encompassed both vital and spiritual health. For only a healthy, read: purified body is able to fulfil its religious duties. Here, the Jewish purity laws are at work that find their equivalent in every washing of the hands before performing a ritual act. Central to Paul is the redemption of the whole human entity, which is entirely saved from death. There is no Greek dualism at work here. The soul, however immortal it may be, is not a separated part of the human being, but an integral part of the individual person and ultimately connected to the Spirit of God. The hope for immortality is not a devaluation of the material word, but a hope for bodily resurrection unknown to Greek thought. God grants immortality through his Spirit, not through the characteristics of the soul. Eternal life in communion with God already begins in earthly life, which points towards the divine.

History of philosophy has often spoken of the soul as the equivalent of personality, the ego and the self. It is a central question whether the human personality, the self, can endure without the body or is only granted through the unity of body and what religion calls soul. Christianity affirms the latter and ties personality to the body-soul unity. The German language knows the distinction between "Leib" and "Körper", which is not transferable to the English language. The former means more than just the physical body and includes the aspect of vitality and conscious existence that we know from Biblical thought. Here the self cannot be experienced and expressed by the soul alone but only through the connection of both parts that form a unity that is more than the parts it consists of. In communication with others, too, it is not the soul alone that enables the self to present itself to the world, but also the body in its capacity as "Leib". The relationship between both is complex and sometimes paradoxical, but again, one cannot state a devaluation of either part, nor the simple congruence of the self with one part or the other. The soul, for example, does not simply enter a body like a vessel in order to find a means of expression.

One specific intermediate approach towards the analysis of the body-soul unity of man is the Aristotelian-Thomistic *hylomorphism*. Using Aristotelian terminology, the "spiritual soul" (*anima rationalis*) is regarded as the substantial form of an individual human being. This *anima* is not pure spirit, but also includes an animalistic and a vegetative dimension. It defines the human being as a *living* being in contrast to mere material. What defines a living *human* being is his possession of a specifically spiritual soul that enables the two parts of *forma* and *materia* to form one specific human being that is inconceivable if one part is missing. No part can exist without the other and thus no part is in itself a human being or an individual self. This self only exists in the interaction of all parts and yet is more than just a sum of its parts. The soul cannot live on immortally as a human "self" without its body. In the human self, in his being alive, *forma* and *materia* are in a certain sense one.

This view was not always common among Christian theologians. It had to prevail against Platonic conceptions that attributed feelings alone to the soul, a soul that makes use of a body. Today, even the Second Vatican Council upholds that a living human being only exists in the unity of *corpus* and *anima*, thus adopting *hylomorphism*. For this reason, man is responsible for his body, which is a gift of God, and has to take care of this important part of his personality.

Christianity thus refuses to split man into two separate parts, one transcendent, one corporeal. This assumption is the result of heavily controversial discussion. *Origen* favoured the pre-existence of all souls, including the soul of Jesus Christ, the only thinkable bearer of the divine logos, which mediates between God and man, finally enabling human nature to become divine. Alexandrian theology, most famously represented by the Patriarch Cyril, assumes that Christ's soul is able to suffer and emphasises the full human nature in Christ, endowed with a self-motion on its own. His opponent, the Antiochenian Nestorius, sees an opposition between the divine *logos* and Christ's human soul. Dogmatic quarrels about the true nature of Christ's soul and their relevance for the salvation of man led to schisms and accusations that lasted for centuries.

Another prominent question was the state of the soul when separated from the body. Normally, this happens in death. What happens to the soul in the intermediate time between death and resurrection? Does it wait for "its" body; can it already enjoy the pleasures of paradise? Is resurrection an individual act that happens in death or do body and soul have to wait for the "other"? Without the union with its body, the soul is deficient. It is no longer called a person. Yet it cannot rot as the body does, which now is a corpse. If it somehow survives death and can glimpse into heaven, some Protestant theologians supposed a platonic remnant, which they wanted to oppose. Thinkers like Karl Barth denied the immortality of the human soul, claiming "total annihilation" in death. An immortal soul would mean a human *hubris* against the new creation that is entirely worked by God's grace. Nothing that was survives death. This ultimately leads to problems, if the risen Christ had no continuity which the woman-born Jesus.

The assumption of an immortal soul has a broader meaning: it speaks of the ultimate standing before the creator, of the final responsibility of the human being created with free will. Life and creation always remain a gift of God and the idea of the existence of a part of the human nature that lasts longer than physical death is a guarantee of the existing connection between God and man.

The unity of body and soul, which is fundamental to Christian thought, has ethical consequences. For man is at the same time bound to transcendence and immanence. The belief in an immortal soul strengthened the idea of the unconditional value of the human life against utilitarian appropriation. The inviolability of the physical human existence is a fundamental philosophical conviction not only since Kant and the Enlightenment. It is not only for theological reasons and the idea of the *imago dei*, the image of God in the human being, that man must possess a human dignity that cannot be ignored or minimised. The body as the only available form of expressing one's own personality, as the only mode of existence that the self can have in the world, must have an intrinsic and undeniable value. This value of the self and the person must be independent from the judgement of others. Its value is not bestowed; it is rather fundamental for human existence. This excludes any discrimination, degradation and devaluation, because belonging to the human species means ultimately consisting of a self that expresses itself with and through its body. The immaterial part of this existence that every man has may be called "soul" in a theological context.

The Concept of Soul in Islam

Just like the other traditions show a multitude of concepts regarding the soul, Islamic thought offers various competing and contradicting concepts of what is described by the Arabic terms *nafs* and *ruh*. As their Hebrew equivalents *nefesh* and *ruaḥ* these terms can describe very different things and are used in many ways. It remains a question of the respective viewpoint if the soul is spiritual or corporeal. Translation is always an approximation to what was meant primarily, and this is especially true for Islam and its central holy scripture, the Qur'an. As the other traditions before Islam, the latter incorporated many thoughts and inquiries by Greek philosophy, Jewish and Christian thought. Islam sees itself as the re-installation of the once uncorrupted religion before Judaism and Christianity failed to keep it true. Therefore, Islam considers itself easily accessible to logical thinking and understanding. No self-contradiction is implied and man must come quite naturally to Islam as the goal of all reasoning. This has also to be true regarding the concept of the soul.

The origins lie in the Greek elaborations whether or not the soul can exist without the body, embodied in the paradigmatic schools of Plato and Aristotle. Both philosophers heavily influenced Islam, as they influenced all major monotheistic religions. From Jewish tradition, Islam borrowed the Old Testament concept of *nefesh*, which refers to the whole entity of the human soul-body connection. A *nefesh* is a living being, a true person and no part can exist without the other. Together with later, Hellenistic speculations about the immortality of the human soul, these currents found their way into Islamic thought. Nevertheless, the question remains open if Islam and especially the Qur'an have a concise concept of the soul.

Islam may see itself as self-explanatory and perfectly reasonable, yet the Qur'an offers a nearly infinite fund of interpretations. There is no real doctrine of the soul. The Jewish *nefesh* appears as *nafs* and represents the whole person, just like in Judaism. God created mankind from one single *nafs*, which is immortal and will eventually face its final judgement. *Nafs* also has a psychological, individual aspect; it represents the personality, the inner being of a human being. The most decisive characteristic is its movement. Islamic thinking knows several successive "states" of the soul, which represent different aspects of human existence and the soul's journey towards God. The soul can be "commanding", i.e. tempting and leading to evil. She can be "blaming", thus repenting her failures. In the end, she may eventually become "tranquillised" and remain in peace with God. Here, all movement ends.

In death, the soul separates from the body and returns to her creator in order to face judgement. Islam knows a broad variety of descriptions of the paradisiacal delights as well as of hellish punishment. Here, the soul is separated from the body, an immortal creation awaiting the final resurrection.

The term *ruh*, on the other hand, denotes the spirit, the breath of life that is given to man, the life force that is breathed into his nostrils. It is not to be confused with the soul. The soul may drive to evil and idleness whereas the breath of life may be harmed by the uncontrolled, daring soul. The soul is attached to the body, thus to the world, and therefore Islamic piety sees a struggle against the temptations of the carnal creation, which is of inferior value, notwithstanding the fact that for the Qur'an, everything God created is good and in itself perfect for man to indulge in it. The soul should love God, not this world. The soul is on a journey towards God and has to leave behind the delights of this world in order to fully embrace its Creator. The number of different states may differ, but consequently the soul that is connected to the body influences the latter in either a positive or a negative way, corresponding to the state of soul it accomplishes. As long as this journey continues, the soul is in motion, which separates it from its origin and final destiny, the motionless tranquillity with God. The soul thus becomes a battleground of desire, repentance and atonement. It longs for its creator, yet is attracted by the pleasures of this word.

Sufism, which is sometimes regarded as Islamic mysticism, knows its own struggles with the soul. It shares no love for this world, but like any mysticism, longs for unification with God. The soul is something with which the mystic has to struggle. Like the above-mentioned commanding soul, the mystic struggles against the pleasures of the senses, against desire and against the resistance to God that the soul invites. It is part of the "great jihad" to fight against one's own soul. The soul is associated with earthly matters, the carnal desires. It is a threat to the spirit, which is pure and God-given. It is necessary to tame the soul in order to find delight in the paradisiacal gardens. The true mystic, however, even renounces the delights of paradise to fully embrace his creator. At the end of the mystical journey the soul no longer has any desire, it is practically dead. Every connection to the world is abandoned. The final stage of the soul, which is often depicted as the "self" of a human being, is to become un-self, to get rid of the self and thus get rid of the soul. Everything else sinks towards God and dissolves in him. At the end of the soul's journey the unification with its creator awaits, the ultimate devotion.

In order to summarize Islamic concepts of the soul one could enlarge the multifarious picture with psychological approaches. Here we find concepts different from theological and mystical speculation. Here, the soul is the representation of the inner state of the human being and not to be separated from the body. In the consummation of wine both body and soul witness changes. All these traditions and different concepts of "soul" agree on some fundamental assumptions: that the soul is related to the body, that it is in itself motion and therefore life and that it undergoes certain changes on its way to God.

Similarities and Differences

If one compares the contributions on the concept of soul in this volume, one immediately notices similarities but also differences between the three monotheistic religions Judaism, Christianity and Islam. Since the similarities are far greater than the divergences, we will begin with them, without concealing the fact that in all three religions the concepts of the soul are of course multi-layered and complex.

In all three major religions of revelation, there is the conviction that, in addition to their physicality, human beings also have a spiritual dimension, which is described by the term "soul" and to which immortality is attributed. This applies at least to rabbinic Judaism, but not to ancient Israel, to which the idea of an immortal soul beyond the human body was still alien, not least because of its strong worldly orientation. Moreover, all three religions have a holistic view of the human being and the completion of the human being is linked to the soul that lives on beyond death.

Due to the close interconnectedness of Judaism and Christianity, it is not surprising that the parallels here are particularly great. In rabbinic Judaism, body and soul form an indissoluble unity not only in this life, but also in the life beyond, in which neither dimension is superior or subordinate to the other. It is the soul-body connection that constitutes the personality of the human being. Such a connection between soul and body, which is contrary to Platonic philosophy, is also assumed in Christianity, where the soul is dealt with above all in patristic and medieval theology. Body and soul are regarded as created by God, whereby according to creatianism the soul of man is not imparted by procreation, but is created by God at this time and inserted into the nascent body. The soul, which is associated with the breath or power of life, is never really separated from the body except in the intermediate state – the promise of resurrection applies to both. In contrast to the Christian view, the soul in Judaism is considered to be created by God in advance.

In Judaism, the time of salvation is tied to the fact that all created souls have lived their lives. On the question of what happens to the soul post-mortem until the final judgement, before which the whole human person must answer, various speculations are found, similar to Christianity, one of them being that it returns to God after death in order to be resurrected with the corresponding body in due course. Especially in the Jewish mysticism of the Middle Ages, there is also the idea that the soul is not completely separated from the body, but that it ascends to a spiritual existence purified from the impurity of the world.

Although both Jewish and Christian thought emphasise the unity of soul and body and assume that both denote the whole human being, Christianity introduces a new aspect with the idea of the sinful depravity or need for redemption of all human beings. However, this does not result in a dualism, as in Greek thought, or in a devaluation of the body, since redemption applies to the whole human being, who is thus promised a bodily resurrection. Although there was always the danger of subordinating the physical to the spiritual, it never prevailed. Furthermore, especially in scholastic theology, the soul is associated with the spirit.

Inasmuch as Islam was influenced by both Judaism and Christianity and, like these two religions, by Greek philosophy, the Islamic concept of the soul is not essentially different from that of Judaism and Christianity. Here, too, instead of dualistic concepts, we find the idea of body-soul unity and the immortality of the soul, which is associated with the breath, breeze or spirit of God and which, according to Islamic mysticism, is on a journey towards unification or merging with God. Since it is threatened in the inner world by various carnal desires, the soul has to answer for itself in judgement. All three monotheistic religions associate the idea of judgement with the idea that both the soul and the body can sin and that both will be separated from each other after death, but will be reunited on the Last Day at the general resurrection of the dead.

The concept of the soul is certainly one of the subjects on which the three religions of revelation differ least.

List of Contributors and Editors

Alan Avery-Peck is Kraft-Hiatt Professor in Judaic Studies at the College of the Holy Cross, Worcester, Massachusetts. He was acting dean of the College of Arts & Sciences at Tulane University from 1990–1992 and Director of the Jewish Studies Program at Tulane University from 1987–1993. He is editor of the *Brill Reference Library of Judaism* and editor-in-chief of *The Review of Rabbinic Judaism*. Among his publications are several translations and commentaries on the Talmud Bavli and Yerushalmi (together with Jacob Neusner), *The Encyclopedia of Religious and Philosophical Writings in Late Antiquity: Pagan, Judaic, Christian* (Leiden and Boston 2007), 467 pp. (co-editor in chief with Jacob Neusner) and "Resurrection of the Body in Early Rabbinic Judaism," in: Tobias Nicklas, Friedrich Reiterer, and Joseph Verheyden, eds., *The Human Body in Death and Resurrection* (Berlin and New York, 2009).

Eberhard Schockenhoff (1953–2020) held the chair for Moral Theology at the University of Freiburg (Breisgau) since 1994. He received his PhD in 1986 and his habilitation in 1989. He was member of the German National Council of Ethics and served as its vice-chairman from 2008–2012. In 2016, he became president of the "Katholischer Akademischer Ausländerdienst" (Catholic Academic Service for Foreigners). From 1995–2005 he was member of the ecumenical commission "Church and justification" for the dialogue between the Lutheran World Federation and the Catholic Church. Eberhard Schockenhoff authored a multitude of books and articles on ethical and theological questions on biological and medical problems such as catholic sexual morality, euthanasia or stem cell research. His last work, *Die Kunst zu lieben: Unterwegs zu einer neuen Sexualethik* (Herder, Freiburg (Breisgau) a. o. 2021), which was released posthumously, dealt with the possibility of a new sexual ethics. Eberhard Schockenhoff died unexpectedly July 18th, 2020.

Bernhard Uhde is Professor Emeritus of Religious Studies and Philosophy of Religions. He habilitated in the field of History of Religions and was Professor of Religious Studies at the University of Freiburg (Breisgau) from 2001–2016. He is Honorary Professor at the Catholic University Freiburg since 2004, at the German University Eriwan (Armenia) since 2011, at the Sulkhan-Saba Orbeliani University Tblisi (Georgia) since 2011 and Honorary Professor at the Pontifical University Lima (Peru) since 2014. In 2015, he founded and headed the "Institute for Interreligious Studies Freiburg". He is the archdiocese's representative for the dialogue with Islam. In 2008, he received the Order of Merit of the Federal Republic of Germany. Among his publications are *Warum sie glauben, was sie glauben. Weltreligionen für Andersgläubige und Nachdenkende* (Freiburg 2013) and *‚Denn Gott ist die Wahrheit' (Koran 22,62). Notizen zum Verständnis von ‚Wahrheit' in der religiösen Welt des Islam* (Freiburg 2011).

Christoph Böttigheimer has held the Chair of Fundamental Theology at the Catholic University of Eichstätt-Ingolstadt since 2002. He studied Catholic theology at the Universities of Tübingen and Innsbruck (Austria), obtained his doctorate at the University of Munich in 1993 and habilitated there in 1996. He is the author of "Lehrbuch der Fundamentaltheologie", one of the most well-received and influential textbooks in the field of fundamental theology in the German-speaking world. His works in the ongoing legacy of the Second Vatican Council, on supplicatory prayer and core questions of faith have been translated into several languages. His most recent publication, besides a new and revised edition of the famous "Lehrbuch", is "Die Reich-Gottes-Botschaft Jesu. Verlorene Mitte christlichen Glaubens" (Freiburg, 2020) on Jesus' teaching in the Kingdom of God. He is

https://doi.org/10.1515/9783110748239-005

member of many academic research and working committees, especially in the field of ecumenical dialogue and cooperation.

Wenzel Maximilian Widenka studied History, Catholic Theology and Interreligious Studies at the Universities of Bamberg and Vienna. He received his PhD in Jewish Studies at the University of Bamberg in 2019 with a study about the struggle for religious emancipation of 19th century Jews on the countryside. He was research assistant at the Chair of Fundamental Theology at the Catholic University of Eichstätt-Ingolstadt and is currently working for a German publishing house specialized in the fields of religion and theology. His most recent publications are "*'Sehet, da kommen Schakale, den Weinberg zu zerstören, den Weinberg Israels.' Emanzipation und Konfessionalisierung im fränkischen Landjudentum in der ersten Hälfte des 19. Jahrhunderts*" (University of Bamberg Press, 2019), as well as "Seinen Namen heiligen, um das Volk zu retten", in: Bruns, Peter / Kremer, Thomas / Weckwerth, Andreas (eds.): *Sterben & Töten für Gott? Das Martyrium in Spätantike und frühem Mittelalter* (Koinonia – Oriens), Münster 2022.

Index of Persons

ʿAbd ar-Raḥīm 105
Abraham 69–70
Abū Ḏarr 96
Abū Ṭālib Muḥammad b. ʿAlī b. ʿAṭīya al-Ḥāriṯī al-ʿAǧami al-Makkī al-Wāʿiẓ *See* al-Makkī
Abū Idrīs al-Ḫawlīnī 96
Abū Saʿīd al-Ḫarrāz 104
Abū Saʿīd b. Abī al-Ḫayr 104
Abū Saʿīd b. al-Aʿrābī 105
Abū Yazīd al-Basṭāmī 105
Abū Zayd Aḥmad b. Sahl al-Balḫī 107
Adam 3, 57, 78, 83, 87, 90
al-Ǧunayd 89
al-Makkī 90–94, 103
Althaus, Paul 53
Apollinaris of Laodicea 50
Aristotle 37, 39, 45, 47–48, 71–74, 76, 81, 83, 99, 122
Arius 52
as-Sarrāǧ 78, 104
ʿAṭṭār 105–107
Augustine 26, 47, 76, 82

Bar Kokhba, Simon 6
Barth, Karl 55, 121
Benedict XII. (Pope) 52
Brunner, Emil 55
Bultmann, Rudolf 31

Cullmann, Oscar 55
Cyprian 82
Cyril of Alexandria 50–52, 121

Derrida, Jacques 79
Descartes, René 44–45, 58
Dumah 13

Enoch 75

Fichte, Johann Gottlieb 55, 58

Gadamer, Hans-Georg 79
Gilson, Etienne 47
Gramlich, Richard 110
Greshake, Gisbert 53, 56

Ḥasan al-Baṣrī 100, 102
Hegel, Georg Wilhelm Friedrich 59
Homer 72
Husserl, Edmund 39

Ibn Rušd 109
Ibrāhīm an-Naẓẓām 85
Isaac Israeli 14
Isaiah 8
ʿIzz ud-dīn Maḥmūd 106

Jacob 4, 70
Jesus Christ 30–31, 34–36, 49–52, 55–56, 70, 81, 85, 87–88, 119, 121
John (evangelist) 36
Judah Halevi 15
Judah the Patriarch 11

Kaiser, Otto 24, 27
Kant, Immanuel 54–55, 58, 121

Locke, John 37

Maḥmūd-i Kāšānī 104
Maimonides 117
Marcel, Gabriel 39, 42
Moltmann, Jürgen 55
Moses 70
Moses Maimonides 15, 117
Muhammad 67, 69–70, 77, 85, 115
Muḥammad al-Ġazzālī 104
Munkar 84, 97

Nakīr 84, 97
Nebuchadnezzar of Babylonia 6
Nestorius 51–52, 121
Nietzsche, Friedrich 40

Odysseus 72
Origen 21, 49–50, 121

https://doi.org/10.1515/9783110748239-006

Patmore, Coventry 98
Paul (apostle) 30–31, 35–36, 119
Pelagius 52
Philo of Alexandria 2, 14
Pieper, Josef 47, 56
Plato 37, 47, 54, 73–74, 76, 81, 115, 122
Plessner, Helmuth 42
Plotinus 47, 76, 99
Priska and Aquila 35
Pseudo-Dionysios Areopagita 98
Pythagoras 73

Ratzinger, Joseph 54
Runggaldier, Edmund 47

Ṣadr ad-Dīn Muḥammad Shīrāzī 110
Sahl at-Tustarī 78
Sahl ibn ʿAbdallāh 94
Schimmel, Annemarie 98
Schnelle, Udo 35
Solomon 6, 75

Tertullian 76
Thomas Aquinas 47–48, 53, 56

ʿUmar b. al-Ḫaṭṭāb 88

Waldenfels, Bernhard 39, 41
Wāṣil b. ʿAṭā' 79
Wetzstein, Verena 62

Index of Subjects

ʿaql 77
anima 2, 25, 34, 47–48, 53, 72, 76, 119–120
anima rationalis 38, 44–45, 120
anima separata 52–53
annihilatio 55, 121
anthropology 21, 23–26, 28, 30–31, 35, 37, 48–49, 53, 57, 118
appetitive soul 81, 103–104

basar 28–30
blaming soul 81–83, 91, 93, 123
body 1, 3–5, 7–18, 21–22, 24–31, 35–48, 51–54, 57–59, 61, 73–74, 80, 83–84, 97, 103, 108, 115–121, 123–125
body-soul unity 22, 24, 27–28, 31, 38, 43–47, 49, 61, 120–121, 124–125
breath of life 3, 22–23, 25, 27, 75, 85, 116, 118, 123

commanding soul 81–83, 87, 89, 92–93, 123
creation 3–4, 8, 17, 22–25, 34, 48, 55–57, 72, 116, 119, 121

death 3–5, 7–8, 12, 14–15, 17–18, 26, 32–36, 52–56, 73, 83–84, 97, 116–119, 121, 123–125

Ecclesiastes 5
El Malé Rahamim 13, 16
entelécheia 73
equivocation 69, 74

fanāʾ 105
flood 27–28
forma 44–45, 47–48, 120
forma substantialis 44

Garden of Eden 9–10, 12–15, 18, 84, 93, 103–104
Gehenna 12, 15, 18
grace 30, 118–119, 121

ḥanīf 70
Hebrew Bible 1–5, 7, 14–15, 22–23, 25, 28, 30–33, 35, 115–116, 118–119, 122
hellenism 2, 22, 28, 33, 35–36, 54, 74, 76, 118–119, 122
hylomorphism 44–48, 52–53, 120–121

image of God 24, 33, 57, 118, 121
immortality 4–5, 8, 13–15, 18, 21, 24, 33, 36, 48, 54–57, 73–74, 76, 84, 115–118, 120–122, 124–125
Israel 2, 6–7, 16–17, 24, 32, 34, 70, 115, 124

Jewish-Roman wars 6, 17, 115

Kabbalah 15, 117
Körper 38–39, 120

leb 27
Leib 38–39, 120

materia 45, 47, 53, 120
messiah 6, 8–9, 28
mysticism 15, 78, 98–105, 110, 123, 125

nafs 67–68, 80–81, 83, 85–86, 107–108, 110, 122
nasḫ 77
nefesh 2–4, 22, 25–28, 35, 74–76, 115, 118–119, 122
neshamah 2, 8, 10–13, 115
New Testament 22, 31, 33–35, 119
noũs 74

Odyssey *See* Odysseus
Old Testament *See* Hebrew Bible
original sin 119
ousía 73

Peri psychês 72–73
person 37–38, 55, 59–62
persuading soul 82, 91, 93
pneuma 27, 30, 119
preexistence (of souls) 9–10, 33, 37
psyché 25–26, 30, 34–35, 72–74, 119

Qur'an 68–71, 77–93, 101, 103, 109–110, 122

https://doi.org/10.1515/9783110748239-007

rabbinic Judaism 6–7, 124
redemption 31, 116, 118
respiration 2–4, 8, 115
resurrection 8, 11, 13, 36, 52–57, 83–84, 117, 120–121, 124–125
revelation 69–70, 77, 79, 124
ruach 2–3, 5, 8–10, 27–28, 74–76, 115–116, 119, 122
rūh 68, 80, 85, 122–123

salvation 21, 23, 28, 31, 33–34, 36, 51, 70, 116, 121
sarx 30–31, 119
Second Vatican Council 48, 57, 120
Shia 67
sin 11–12, 30–31, 87, 90–92, 117, 119
soma 30–31, 74, 119
soul 1–5, 7–18, 21–22, 24–30, 32–38, 40, 44–58, 60–62, 67, 72–76, 80–84, 86, 88–89, 94–97, 102–108, 110–111, 115–118, 120–125
spiritus 2, 27, 119
Sufism 100–102, 104, 110, 123
sunna 67

taḥrīf 70
Talmud 7–9, 11–12, 14, 116–117
temple 6–7, 115–116
total death 55
tranquillised soul 82–83, 89–91, 93–94, 123
translation 68–69
Tree of Zaqqūm 84

univocation 69

yetser ha-ra 82
yetser ha-tov 82

www.ingramcontent.com/pod-product-compliance
Lightning Source LLC
Chambersburg PA
CBHW031403230426
43670CB00006B/629
* 9 7 8 3 1 1 0 7 4 8 1 8 5 *